"Over the many years that I have know appreciated his wisdom and reflectior words, books, and regular blog posts). followed his writings. *Wisdom's Way tc* endeavors for which I, and I believe anyone, will be wiser and happier for having read it."

— **Jonathan Myers, PhD,** Research Scientist, Stanford University

"This book is to the point and inspirational, making it a powerful and easy read. It's filled with great advice and simple actions to take. You will find it both enjoyable and practical."

— **Sue Anderson,** Vie, Founder & CEO

"Dave Jensen has been my coach and mentor for nearly 30 years. This wonderful compendium is a delightful consolidation of Dave's many passions, his endless pursuit of truth, his openness to feedback, his study of philosophy, and his absolute commitment to using compelling research to inform his teaching and his life. I think this volume should be on everyone's bedside table to remind us daily of our opportunities to search for and work toward the best life has to offer."

— **Mary Rose Patejak,** Executive Director Finance, University of Southern California Care

"*Wisdom's Way to Happiness Today* is a must-read! In this book, Dave Jensen combines a friendly writing style, decades of research, and an insatiable pursuit of the truth to bring you everyday practical applications that can improve your life. You will gain insights to enhance your decision-making and maximize your happiness journey as you bask in the wisdom of Dave's leadership."

— **Jodi Walker,** Chief Creative Catalyst, Success Alliances

"*Wisdom's Way to Happiness Today* is a guidebook providing readers with realworld tools for growth, decision-making, and happiness. It is my good fortune to be friends with the author. From that point of view, I can assure you that Dave Jensen fully utilizes the methods and guidance he offers, in his own life. He is a teacher and perpetual student. This book is based on his sincere desire to help others. I believe he has done just that!"

— **Jim Montgomery,** President, Diagnostic Specialties

WISDOM'S
WAY
to Happiness Today

DAVID G. JENSEN

WISDOM'S
WAY
to Happiness Today

DAVID G. JENSEN

**WORLD
BUSINESS
PUBLISHING**

To my students *who teach me so much.*

To my friends *who help me up.*

To my family *who welcomes me home.*

Wisdom's Way to Happiness Today
by David G. Jensen
World Business Publishing
3518 Barry Ave.
Los Angeles, CA 90066
Design & Text Composition by Steve Rachwal
Manufactured in the United States of America
Publishers Cataloging-in-Publication Data
Jensen, David.
Wisdom's Way to Happiness Today / David G. Jensen.
p. cm.
Includes bibliographical references and index.
1. Leadership 2. Management I. Title
Library of Congress Control Number:
ISBN 978-0-578-93302-3

Table of Contents

Wisdom Shines Its Light Where Knowledge and Experience Unite

« Let no one be slow to seek wisdom when he is young,

Nor weary in the search of it when he has grown old.

For no age is too early or too late for the health of the soul. »

EPICURUS

I sat on the ground, leaning against the giant oak tree in our Connecticut backyard. I opened my book of stories to a random page, as was my custom at that time, and read by the full moon's light. This was the night I learned that King Solomon didn't pray for riches, honors, or a long life. He prayed only for the wisdom to lead his life and his people well.

WOW, I thought, gazing up at the moon. *Seeking only wisdom. What else do you really need when you have wisdom?* At the tender age of fifteen, I decided I wanted wisdom too. I've been searching for it ever since.

Smart Is Not Wise

To have wisdom is to *have the knowledge and experience to live well.* By definition, being wise is not the same as being smart. There are many types of smart, but it is most often associated with having facts. Wisdom, on the other hand, is concerned with integrating facts with experience to make quality life decisions that lead to living well. As a leadership educator and coach, I have traveled extensively throughout America for more than three decades. Although I found most people smart enough, I saw the damage done by a deficit of wisdom. I also see it today in politics, on the news, and in my own neighborhood.

Thirty years ago, when I was teaching a workshop in Silicon Valley, I met a very smart computer programmer. I'll call him Dan. (The stories are real, although the names are not.) He invited me to lunch, and I remember thinking, *This guy is brilliant.* During subsequent conversations, I learned Dan had scored perfectly on his SATs and was a member of MENSA (the club for those with extremely high IQs). We stayed in touch for several years. Sadly, I watched him get fired from one job after another. His intelligence had morphed into narrow-mindedness. Lessons from experience went unlearned. I tried to coach Dan, to no avail. Last I heard, he was living in an assisted living facility for low-income seniors.

« When he told me how smart he was,
I wondered where his wisdom went. »

Dan is an example of a very smart person lacking the wisdom to make quality decisions. Haven't you seen intelligent people do dumb things…over and over again? Smart is not enough. This book will show you how to gain wisdom in a month.

Wisdom's Way in Thirty-two Days

No matter where you are on the wisdom scale, and you're about to discover where that is, my intention is for this book to help you boost your wisdom in at least three ways. First, it will improve your decision-making. We all make decisions all day, every day. Each of us is, in fact, a decision-making factory. Yet few of us have ever learned an evidence-based decision-making process. This book won't tell you *what* to think; it will reveal *how* to frame your micro and macro thinking to make wise decisions.

The second way this book will turbo-charge your wisdom is by showing you how to avoid the seduction of fleeting pleasures as you pursue life's meaningful treasures. You'll see how the wise enjoy short-term gratification without compromising long-term life satisfaction.

A third way these pages will elevate your wisdom is by helping you cope with the pain of life's heartaches. While our pain is a given, suffering can be an option. The wise learn to see setbacks as feedback waiting for meaning.

« Life can only be understood backwards;
but it must be lived forwards. »

SØREN KIERKEGAARD

Experience Drenched by Research

Since Solomon touched my teenage soul long ago, I have tried to gain the knowledge and experience that would blossom into wisdom. My journey has not been direct or easy, nor has it always led to wisdom or happiness. I've lost my way, wandered astray, and fallen on so many days. Despite these missteps, and perhaps because of them, I sojourned on with a prayer in my heart, service in my soul, and a burning desire to grow.

I must admit it's humbling to think I have wisdom to share. Yet, as I gaze back on my life, I see a unique blend of knowledge and experience drenched by decades of research that have given me unique insights that may be useful to others. For example, over the last fifty years, I have:

1. Juggled three jobs simultaneously to pay my way through high school and college

2. Listened to mentors who nudged me out of factory jobs into graduate school

3. Worked with world-renowned scientists when I interned at UCSD

4. Conducted and published research for five years when hired by UCSD

5. Became a top salesperson for a medical equipment company

6. Accepted an executive position at UCLA

7. Started my own consulting/training firm thirty years ago

8. Authored evidence-based books on leadership and sales

9. Taught at Rockhurst College, Emory University, and TEDx

10. Educated thousands of participants throughout the US in my workshops

11. Digested thousands of research articles on happiness, sales, leadership, philosophy

12. Surrounded myself with wise friends who challenged my thinking

13. Overcame family tragedies and three near-death experiences

14. Reflected on my many missteps and other life lessons by journaling for thirty years

These experiences, combined with my lifelong quest for knowledge, blossomed into this book—a practical guide to wisdom. Although I am the author, I owe an enormous debt of gratitude to so many people, especially the thousands of individuals I have taught. I've learned so much from my students. You are about to learn not only from my experiences but from the experiences I gleaned from them. When the *teacher* was ready, the students appeared. The participants in my many classes, workshops, and seminars showed up year after year. Their wit and wisdom are beneath the words you read here.

> « *Of all the pursuits open to men, the search for wisdom is most perfect, more sublime, more profitable, and more full of joy.* »
>
> THOMAS AQUINAS

How Wise Are You Now?

The journey of wisdom starts where you are. Thus, our adventure begins today by assessing how wise you are right now by taking the Wisdom Insight Quiz.* I developed this scale after reviewing many wisdom assessments and selecting only ten statements that predict wisdom. The excellent review by Sai-fu Fung and colleagues was most helpful.* Score the following ten statements on a scale of 1 *(strongly disagree)* to 5 *(strongly agree)*. Don't overanalyze them. Answer them quickly and honestly from your gut:

1. I often feel real compassion for everyone.

2. I frequently laugh at my little mistakes and use humor to put others at ease.

3. I enjoy being around others whose views are strongly different from mine.

4. I have a deep desire to understand the truth.

5. I am not easily irritated by people who argue with me.

6. I like to recall my past to provide perspective on current concerns.

7. I make important decisions after gathering facts and considering diverse opinions.

8. I often wonder about the mysteries of life and what lies beyond death.

9. I easily express my emotions without losing control.

10. I have learned from many painful events in my life.

*Sai-fu Fung, Esther Oi-wah Chow, and Chau-kiu Cheung, Development and validation of a brief self-assessed wisdom scale, *BMC Geriatrics* 20, no. 54 (2020).

Your Wisdom Score

1. Add up your answers to generate your wisdom score.

2. Plot your score on the Wisdom Insight Continuum below.

3. Plot where you would like to be on the continuum.

4. Decide which of the ten statements need to improve to get you where you want to go.

Unwise	Narrow-minded	Open-minded	Mindful	Wise
10	20	30	40	50

The difference between where your score is now (current state) and where you want it to be (desired state) is your gap. Don't worry about how big your gap is. What you say about it is more important than its width. When the wise see the size of their gap, they simply say it's time to build my bridge today.

How to Use This Book to Build Your Wisdom Bridge

The title of each chapter is one of my favorite quotations. I say "my" quotations because, over the last three decades, these quotes came to me, usually while I was teaching, talking with friends, or cycling up steep mountain roads. I've written and archived hundreds of them. The ones in this book are the best. I have done my due diligence to see if these quotes "belonged" to anyone else. My research indicated that the answer is no. However, I've been influenced by so many people for so many years, I don't claim exclusive authorship of these quotes. So, let me know if you discover that the quote is by someone else. Also, feel free to use "my" quotes without attributing them to me.

I recommend that you read one chapter a day for a month to get the most out of the book. (In all, you'll find thirty-two chapters, which will be helpful to you if you are reading this book in a leap year.) Most chapters are only a few pages. However, there are a few chapters that are a page or two longer. I let the chapters tell me how long they needed to be. Each chapter tells a short story that explores the meaning of that chapter's quote, why it's relevant, and how to adapt the lesson to boost your wisdom. The stories are as real as fading memories permit. The names have been changed. Read each chapter like you're drinking a glass of fine wine. Take it in slowly. Savor whatever bubbles up for you, including a rejection of the chapter's wisdom. You may want to discuss these ideas with your friends, family, and colleagues. When you finish a chapter, decide what ideas might work for you, how to test-drive them, and leave the rest on the cutting-room floor. Then, conduct your own little experiment. Action is the essence of commitment.

You may notice some overlap among the chapters discussing free will, choice, and the meaning of life. They teach similar principles from different perspectives. They also present the most powerful lessons from my life.

It is also true that a few chapters discuss concepts that are common sense. But just because ideas are common sense doesn't mean they lack wisdom. Each chapter is here because it needs to be more common out there—in the real world. If you disagree, that's great. Take what fits you the best and forget about the rest.

If you read and apply one chapter a day for one month, I believe you'll experience the joy of building bridges that span your wisdom gap.

Singing Words of Wisdom

Several chapters conclude with lyrics. Yes...lyrics! As I drafted the book, I discovered these lyrics popping up and capturing the essence of the chapter. I have never written poetry or songs before. Nor am I a musician. Yet, when I searched my heart, a voice in my head said to share the wisdom through these lyrics. So that's what I've done.

Music can be a sound way to spread healing to those who are hurting. Like a lighthouse during a storm, songs have the power to shine a light for those adrift at night. But lyrics need melodies to show the way. I'm still trying to figure out that part. What do you say? Who do you know? I'm open to the possibilities of *rock-and-soul*.

CHAPTER 1

Pursue What Is True

Hal stood in the corner of the small dining room, his nose tilted up, shoulders back, chest out, rigid, like a royal guard at Buckingham Palace. Above the joyful din of our holiday party, I could hear Hal arguing his "case," having something to do with engineering.

The Arrogance of Ignorance

What does Hal know about engineering? He's a lawyer. I mumbled to myself. *AND why is he arguing with George, who IS an engineer?* I slid past a few friends to eavesdrop as Hal pressed his opinion. George sighed as he explained one last time where Hal's thinking was flawed. But Hal would have none of it. His face flushed red, nostrils flared, until through clenched teeth, Hal growled his closing argument. George shrugged, "Whatever you say, Hal," then he waltzed across the room to the buffet table overflowing with holiday treats.

By this time, I wanted to shout, "Hey Hal, you're a smart lawyer, but you have lost your wisdom...again! Where's your evidence, proof, facts to back up your argument?" But I chose to keep my own counsel and instead wandered over to those holiday treats, wondering, *Is dogma the megaphone of the weak?*

Hal didn't have any evidence. No data to support his tunnel-vision view on this topic. Hal was ignorant like we all are on certain issues. Worse than ignorance was Hal's disinterest in seeking the truth. He refused to "Pursue what is true." Instead, his arrogance of ignorance fueled his overconfidence.

> *« Just because you're wrong*
> *doesn't make me right. »*

There Is a House...

Imagine you and Hal are standing next to each other outside a large house. As you both peer through the same window, Hal starts describing what's happening in other rooms. You ask how he knows what's going on in other parts of the house. He becomes defensive and starts justifying his views. Hal then refuses your invitation to walk around to gain different perspectives. Because you are on the path of wisdom, you sigh and calmly wave goodbye.

To obtain the knowledge needed to grow wisdom, we must first recognize that "we live on an island of knowledge surrounded by a sea of ignorance," as physicist John Archibald Wheeler pointed out. Wisdom blooms in the rich soil of humility and receptivity. Wisdom is seldom about having the answer; more often than not, it's about pursuing it. To grow wise is a daily journey of discovery, grounded in the understanding that what we see is shaped by where we stand.

Hal was smart but lacked wisdom, much like Dan, my MENSA friend discussed in the introduction. Neither Hal nor Dan pursued what was true because they believed their view was the only view. They had not learned that most dogma is dog pooh. Those who are wise invite discussions about perceptions. They stroll around the house knowing that diverse views help everyone see the big picture, often leading to better decisions.

> *« It isn't what we don't know that gives us*
> *trouble, it's what we know that ain't so. »*

Attributed to MARK TWAIN

Now I'm a Believer

It's easy to be deceived by what we believe because our beliefs are defined, refined, and streamlined throughout our lives. We become what we believe. Our beliefs serve us well…most of the time. When they become too rigid, however, they become blinders.

For example, a few years ago, I was reading an article by a politician who advocated major cuts in the military budget. Since I believe in a strong military, I was about to stop reading and dismiss the politician's biased argument when I realized that clinging to my belief in this moment would be like Hal refusing to walk around the house. So, I took a deep breath, reminded myself to pursue what is true, and took off my blinders. That's when I discovered how big the US yearly military budget is when *compared to other countries.*

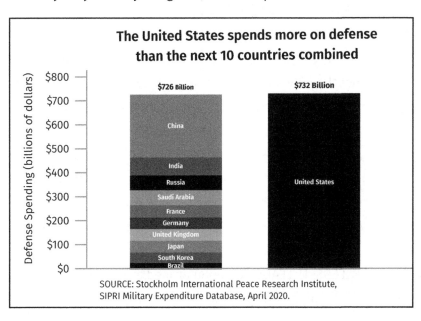

The United States spends more on defense than the next 10 countries combined

SOURCE: Stockholm International Peace Research Institute, SIPRI Military Expenditure Database, April 2020.

While the chart shown here may be a bit dated, insight gleaned from seeing the proportion is still relevant. The US military budget is greater than the next ten largest countries' military budgets combined. *What?* I thought to myself, *I had no idea our military budget was THAT huge compared to other countries.* Nor did I know that we have 600+ military bases in sixty countries. I was shocked by the size of the US military budget and my ignorance of these facts.

By the way, I'm not proposing to cut the military budget. I'm not even suggesting you do anything with these facts at this time. I *am* confessing that I almost skipped reading an illuminating article because of my biased beliefs. I almost chose not to *pursue what is true*. When does this happen to you?

« *A strong belief
will defeat an army of facts.* »

I Saw the News Today, Oh Boy

If you tune into Fox or CNBC, you'll also see that they pretend to *tell* us the news when they are really *selling* us their one-sided views. They are not the only ones. Many popular media pundits push their polarized opinions. But have you ever wondered why so many people buy what they're selling? Three reasons: First, our brain is lazy. Ironically, the brain's mandate is, DON'T MAKE ME THINK! It loves to conserve energy, which enables the brain's survival subroutines to look out for danger. This is why it's easier to buy what someone is selling us than it is to search for evidence, ponder the facts, and come to our own conclusions.

IF IT BLEEDS, IT LEADS is a popular media mantra that reveals the second reason we often buy what others are selling: Our brain's programming pushes us to take fast, energy-conserving shortcuts when we perceive danger. Our brain's evolutionary impulse is to survive by reacting, not reflecting. Of course, this is the proper response if lions are chasing us. But when the media feeds us a steady diet of fear-based news, the emotional center of our brain (i.e., amygdala) hijacks our thinking part of the brain (i.e., cerebral cortex). If we are constantly bombarded with messages of danger, we start believing that kittens are lions.

The third reason we often buy what the biased pundits sell us is that misery loves company. Social media makes it easy for us to find and follow "friends" who hold similar views. The social media algorithms keep feeding us who and what to follow, reinforcing a narrow view. These echo chambers create a feeling of belonging that is often exploited to foster victim thinking and the *us* versus *them* narrative.

How to Be an Open-Minded Skeptic

To overcome our brain's desire to buy what the biased pundits sell, we must become "open-minded skeptics." An open-minded skeptic knows that their own beliefs can cause them to overfocus on information, data, and facts that support only their view. Thus, they appreciate thoughtful perspectives that challenge their beliefs. They welcome a walk around the house to discuss what others see. Open-minded skeptics also pursue what is true by seeking unbiased news (e.g., allsides.com).

« *To pursue what is true
grows the wisdom in you.* »

Hal, the smart yet unwise lawyer in this chapter's opening story, sat alone in a corner that evening. I think he would have been much happier at the holiday party, and perhaps in life, had he followed the three Be's of open-minded skeptics:

1. **Be strong enough to doubt your beliefs.**

2. **Be curious enough to explore diverse perspectives.**

3. **Be humble enough to change your mind.**

Don't be like Hal. Find ways to remind yourself to practice these three "Be's" daily. Insert them in your calendar, write them on a Post-it note, make them an agenda item in your meetings, implore friends to remind you to "Be" an open-minded-skeptic. You'll soon see that happiness blooms where wisdom grows.

« Keep the company of those who seek the truth;
run from those who have found it. »

VACLAV HAVEL

Pursue What Is True

I thought we came to share our light,
A café connection felt so right.
I didn't know the darkness would dine
With us that night.

I missed the signs; my cup was full.
Your smile without eyes was a frown still.
I listened but I didn't hear
The meaning below your words, I fear.

Sorry, I missed every clue,
What did I say that wounded you?
If deep, dark questions lie inside,
Stars can't shine on blackened skies.
Won't you pursue what is true?

Check landed fast, time to pay
We shuffled out of the noisy café.
You grabbed the rail, I still didn't know
This time you were letting me go.

I drove you to depart and fly.
I pulled your baggage, heard you sigh.
Your Hollywood hug said goodbye.
Mute is the shadow's loudest lie.

Sorry I missed every clue,
What did I say that wounded you?
If deep, dark questions lie inside,
Stars can't shine on blackened skies.
Won't you pursue what is true.

The sun set on your westward flight.
I turned east toward the city lights.
Truth dawned in me late that night:
Without questions, there's no light.

We all should pursue what is true;
With friends, neighbors, strangers too.
Ask clear questions, don't be deceived
By misty feelings or blind beliefs.
To pursue what is true, sets us free.

And we won't go wrong when we live the song.

CHAPTER 2

Be Open to Most, Attached to Few

Down by the River

Seven monks marched down the well-worn path through the dark forest. Their heads bowed in silent prayer. They were on their annual pilgrimage, purifying their minds and renewing their vows.

Suddenly, they heard a cry in the wilderness. Peering through the trees, the seven monks saw a young woman sobbing on the banks of the river. Her milky white skin glistened in the late-afternoon sun as tears streamed down her swollen cheeks.

Six wide-eyed monks looked away quickly and raced past the damsel in distress. But the seventh left the path, hiked down the embankment, and sat next to the young maiden.

"Why are you crying, my child?" the monk asked, breaking his vow of silence.

"I must cross the river to continue my journey, but I'm afraid I might drown." She whimpered.

"Let me help you." The monk scooped her up in his arms tenderly, waded across the waist-deep river, and put her down gently. The grateful woman thanked him profusely. His soft eyes and open heart smiled in return. The monk crossed the river again and rejoined his six brothers. All seven continued their silent sojourn.

That night, after their simple meal, the seventh monk slept peacefully while the other six tossed and turned.

As dawn's light streaked through the forest the next morning, the monks ate their biscuits, rolled their blankets, and resumed their journey. By midday, the six monks were about to burst. They stopped and confronted the seventh monk: "Why did you break your vows of silence and purity by carrying that woman across the river?"

The monk scanned their furrowed brows and confessed, "Yes, I left our path to help a troubled woman follow hers. I also set her down yesterday. Why do you still carry her today?"

Expect the Best

This seventh monk was reminding his six brothers that happiness comes to those who follow three principles. The first? Expect the best every day. Those who expect the best from themselves and others tend to get the best. This principle works the other way, too. Those who consciously or subconsciously expect the worst often attract negativity into their lives. Every year, the seven monks prayed for a fulfilling journey. This year was no different. Their optimistic attitude was a wonderful way to start their journey. But it was not enough to complete their journey.

Be Open to Most

The second key to happiness is to be open to most experiences that come our way. For example, I have biked up the same Santa Monica mountain roads every weekend for more than thirty years. Each ride is unique because I try to be aware of my experience as I have it. I'm mindful of the flowers blooming over there, hawks arguing with the crows overhead, and the powerful legs of the cyclists who just passed me. I'm also mindless at times. As I ride, I let my thoughts drift like wispy clouds above. The creative dance of being mindful and mindless has helped me to be open to new situations that have taken me out of my routine...which is what a horse did many years ago. Let me explain.

Once upon a time, as I was straining to reach the top of my favorite mountain, I heard the white horse, Quasar, in his corral snorting loudly. I hopped off my bike and walked over to him to say hello. Instead of trotting away, like he had done every time before, this time Quasar pranced across his coral to greet me. He nodded his head up and down and, to my astonishment, let me pet him. Every weekend after that, for the next ten years, when Quasar saw me cycling up his steep, lonely road, he trotted across his corral, waited for me to hop off my bike, and to pet and feed him...with an apple from my cycling jersey.

One gray day in May, Quasar's corral was empty, as it was the following weekend, and the next, and the next...Quasar had died. Sadness filled my heart as I rode past his deserted coral over the next several weeks. The song "Puff the Magic Dragon" played in my head.

Six of the seven monks were not open to what was happening right before their eyes. They couldn't see the woman's plight because they wouldn't look beyond their vows. They worshipped their vows instead of what their vows stood for. To adhere to rigid rituals without acting on what they stand for is unwise. The six monks missed a chance to serve their higher purpose. Only the seventh monk saw that what was before him...was for him.

« What is before us is for us. »

Be Attached to Few

As I reflect on Quasar's passing, I know I never would have had ten years of joy with him had I not been open to interrupting my cycling routine by trying something new: being with Quasar.

After the seventh monk ferried the fair maiden across the river, he put her down. He released his experience like a leaf drifting downstream. He practiced the third key of happiness—knowing when to let go. He turned his attention back to his vows of silence and purity of mind as soon as he rejoined the other six. They, on the other hand, let the experience hold them back. They marched ahead but stared behind.

Resentments, hurts, disappointments, mistakes, and detours pile on as we march through life. Of that, there is no question. The question is: *Once we have a challenging experience, how long do we let it have us?*

To ruminate about the past carries that past into our present, which can burden our future. It's unwise to allow the past to rob our future. The seventh monk reminds us that every day ends at midnight and that happiness dawns on those who let bygones be gone.

These three simple happiness steps are summarized in the "Happiness Equation" seen below.

The Happiness Equation
Happiness = Experience − Expectations

This equation reveals that **our happiness with any experience is equal to how we perceive that experience minus our expectations before the experience.** For example, think about an event or incident when you were disappointed (e.g., slow service at an expensive restaurant, long lines at your grocery store, a lousy movie). On a scale of 1 to 10, what score would you assign your expectations *before* your experience? (Go ahead; pick a high number if you had high hopes. I'll use 8 for this example.) Next, on a scale of 1 to 10, what score would you assign the experience *after* it was delivered? (Pick a low number if you had a terrible experience. I'll use 2.). If you do the math (2 − 8), you generate a "happiness score" (−6). If the number is negative, you are unhappy. If it's positive, you're happy. If it's 0, you're satisfied because your experience matched your expectations.

At first glance, it appears that the equation instructs us to have low expectations before any experience. Haven't you heard some form of the old saying, "Have no expectations and you won't be disappointed"? Although there is some truth in this statement, it neglects the avalanche of evidence that concludes high expectations fuel high performance. This is the so-called *Pygmalion effect* or self-fulfilling prophecy. That's why it's wise to have high expectations *before* any experience and then let go of those expectations *during* and *after* the experience. As our minister once proclaimed, *"That which has come to pass, has come to pass...so let it pass."*

Gimme Three Steps

The Happiness Equation illustrates how you can live happily ever after...one experience at a time, if you take these three steps:

1. Have grand expectations before any experience. Expect the best to increase the odds you'll experience the best.

2. Release your expectations as your experience begins. Be present for your experience as it unfolds for you.

3. Make meaning out of your experience afterward. Brainstorm answers to this question: *How might I think about this in a positive light?*

> « *Resentment is my attachment*
> *to unfulfilled expectations.* »

The Happiness Equation will help you to *be open to most, attached to few*. Keep the equation in front of you as a daily cue. Test-drive it with friends. The lyrics about seven monks can also serve as a reminder....

Open to Most, Attached to Few

Seven monks marched through the woods,
Heads bowed with sacred vows.
Stunned by a woman's cry,
Six wide-eyed monks plowed on.
One felt her plea, went to see
Her tears, a rising stream.
Lifting her tenderly,
One carried her cross...
So she could follow her dream.

> *Open to most,*
> *Attached to few:*
> *Yesterday had its time with you.*
> *Open to most,*
> *Attached to few:*
> *Today's present gift is here for you.*

One rejoined the other six,
Those vexed by her sight.
Six monks tossed and turned,
Lust haunts dark nights.
All marched ahead, six stared behind
Stuck on One broke vow.
But when six howled, One smiled loud:
I carried her once,
Yet you still carry her now.

> **Open to most,**
> **Attached to few:**
> **Yesterday had its time with you.**
> **Open to most,**
> **Attached to few:**
> **Today's present gift is here for you.**

Six monks woke at dawn,
Heard the word One prayed.
Souls lit by vows of truth,
Vibrate namaste:

> This day I live on purpose,
> My heart's a beacon now.
> I drop rusty chains of old
> The past won't hold me down.
> I soar among green forest,
> Walk on leaves turned to brown.
> Cross streams for those dreams
> Once lost, today they're found.

So open to most,
Attached to few:
The past had its time with you.
Open to most,
Attached to few:
Now, here, this—your gift to you.

CHAPTER 3

When the Future Is Foggy, Camp

"Which of these rivers was the Missouri?" That was the question Meriwether Lewis wrote in his journal and discussed with William Clark in June 1805. American explorers Lewis and Clark followed President Thomas Jefferson's orders for more than a year: "The object of your mission is to explore the Missouri River...." But now they were stumped by a fork in that river. So they camped. Over the next few days, the leaders ordered the men to measure the size of the two rivers, detail the characteristics of their waters, and explore the upper reaches of both. Lewis and Clark then met with their men, reviewed the evidence, and listened to their opinions before deciding which river to follow. They chose wisely.

This episode of Lewis and Clark's expedition teaches us that *when the future is foggy, camp.* More specifically, whenever you are in uncharted terrain, Lewis and Clark can show us *how* to camp:

Stop—press your internal pause button.

Look—scan your environment to assess options.

Listen—consider who might help you decide how to proceed.

Should I Stay or Should I Go Now?

Several years ago, I found myself in unfamiliar territory. A client hired me to teach a topic she thought I knew very well. I didn't tell her I was not an expert because I felt I could come up to speed quickly over the next few months. We agreed to proceed. What a mistake! I won't trouble you with the unpleasant details, other than to say that the session did not go well. In fact, it went so poorly that when the client asked for my invoice, I told her that there would be no charge. It's the only time in my career that I felt I did not earn my fee. I failed to deliver a quality workshop because, unlike Lewis and Clark, I didn't *Stop, Look, and Listen.*

> « *Lost is when the map in your head doesn't match the environment.* »

When the future is foggy, the Stop, Look, and Listen philosophy grounds us so we don't become lost in a fantasy. Had I stopped, looked closely at my lack of expertise, and listened to the input of experienced colleagues, I think I would have made a much better decision and referred this client to a real expert.

If Lewis and Clark decided too quickly, they could have spent too much time wandering in the mountains instead of marching toward the Pacific Ocean. On the other hand, if they decided too slowly, they might have been trapped in the clutches of the mountain's severe winter. Either of the extremes would have jeopardized their mission.

Successful leaders like Lewis and Clark make good decisions when facing a foggy future because they know how to camp. Now, you do too. I encourage you to practice these three steps (*Stop, Look, and Listen)* whenever you face a foggy future.

Speaking of practice...yes, we're talking about practice...the next chapter discusses a wise way to practice, practice, practice.

CHAPTER 4

Practice Doesn't Make Perfect, Progressive Practice Makes Progress

Stand and Deliver

My heart was racing, my breathing was shallow, and my mouth was dry. I was confident in my data but not in my presentation skills. Yet, here I was, a twenty-seven-year-old researcher at the University of California–San Diego (UCSD) Medical Center about to present my controversial research to a crowded room of world-renowned physicians, professors, and scientists. Yikes!

I took a deep breath and proceeded to step through my slides (yes, actual slides, not PowerPoint). Before you could say *in conclusion,* I was showing my last slide summarizing my contentious findings: *the new technique did NOT work!* One of our own highly esteemed scientists, Bill, who was sitting in the front row, had developed the new technique. Yet here I was, showing data that directly contradicted Bill's published research.

The audience of distinguished faculty challenged me with difficult but fair questions. I stood tall as I answered them all. Our cardiology department chairperson concluded the meeting by thanking me for an excellent presentation and encouraging Bill to visit our lab to discover why my results conflicted with his. Bill slumped in his chair, forced a fake smile, and assured everyone that he would visit our lab to investigate. He never came, despite my numerous calls.

Feedback Keeps Us on Track

I share this story because it illustrates the wisdom in understanding that *practice doesn't make perfect; progressive practice makes progress.* These are the four simple steps you can take whenever you want to develop a new skill:

1. **Try the new skill in the right environment.** I joined Toastmasters International to boost my overall public speaking skills.

2. **Gather accurate and progressive feedback about your attempts.** I practiced my presentations dozens of times on my own and then solicited feedback from several close colleagues.

3. **Make course corrections based on what you learn.**

4. **Try, try again…and again!** I asked a few senior researchers who tended to be more critical to help me. And I improved with each practice session.

Things get better when we grow bigger. I'm convinced that employing these four principles played a significant role in persuading our faculty that my findings, not Bill's, were correct. The director of our UCSD research team taught us that progressive practice was critical to good science. He created a culture that respected honest, direct, and constructive feedback. This environment contributed to our success, much like it has for a phenomenally successful movie studio....

To Infinity and Beyond

The movie studio Pixar has created a string of twenty-three block-buster films (*Toy Story, Inside Out, The Incredibles,* to name a few) unmatched in the film industry. One of the keys to Pixar's extraordinary success is its "brain trust." When directors want helpful feedback, they invite the brain trust to view their work in progress. The session is a two-hour give-and-take discussion focused on one goal: *provide input to make a better movie.* Egos, titles, and thin skins are left at the door. Directors claim these sessions produce progress because the candid feedback is from expert colleagues who collaborate in a spirit of trust. After the meeting, the director of the movie decides what feedback to accept or reject. Pixar's culture, like ours at UCSD, celebrates progressive practice.

I'm thankful to the thousands of participants who have given me insightful evaluations and the hundreds of brilliant colleagues who critiqued my teaching over the last three decades. Their wise feedback has helped me grow my skills and achieve many goals. I encourage you to apply the four steps of progressive practice to develop your skills. If appropriate, cultivate a learning culture that supports this approach because, as we'll discuss in the next chapter, culture is the great feedback system.

CHAPTER 5

Culture Is the Great Feedback System

"Oh, Dave, did that hurt?" My grandfather grinned, seeing that I stabbed my thumb with the fishing hook.

"Yes, Ole." My eight-year-old voice cracked as tears welled up, and a small bubble of blood oozed.

"Well, if you want sympathy, look up S.H.I.T. in the dictionary. It's right before sympathy."

• • •

What kind of response is that from a kid's grandfather? But that was Ole, our wonderful, cold, stoic grandfather.

That little incident provides a keyhole view of our family dynamics. My three brothers, sister, and I received little in the way of sympathy or displays of affection growing up. It was part of our family's culture.

We Long to Belong

Humans are social animals, which is why most of us like to be members of many groups. Be they families, clubs, teams, organizations, nationalities, or entire nations, most folks feel the magnetic pull to be members of various and numerous tribes. We long to belong. Culture is the set of implicit beliefs and values that describes "the way things are done around here." They are the behaviors that are acceptable to a group. Culture is the feedback process that defines the norms of inclusion and exclusion. It's the cookbook describing *how* to belong.

I've felt the power of culture as it shaped my family's behaviors, as illustrated in my fishing tale with Ole. I've also seen culture shape behaviors when I worked for global giant XYZ. I applauded our company when we purchased a small, entrepreneurial company (EC) to boost our computer product line. But I mourned as I saw our calcified culture crush EC's creative spirit. EC employees tried to cling to their own small group culture, to no avail. Over time, the most talented EC employees marched out because they didn't fit in. They told me that they felt constrained by XYZ's bureaucratic policies, procedures, and protocols. Fitting in made them feel small.

Culture Clash

When a large group pressures a smaller group to conform to its culture, the small group often feels threatened, causing that small group to cling more tightly to their own "way of life." The larger group then pushes harder for conformity, while the smaller group struggles to keep their own identity. This is what happened at XYZ and is the essence of most culture wars.

Culture wars are seldom settled peacefully because neither side defines the problem accurately. When there is a clash of two cultures, you do not have a problem to solve. Rather, you have a paradox to manage. A paradox is when two competing goals pull you in opposite directions at the same time. For example, in the XYZ/EC story, if company executives had diagnosed their issue as a paradox, they would have understood that they had two conflicting goals:

A. Support the small group's (EC's) entrepreneurial culture.

AND at the Same Time

B. Embrace the large group's (XYZ's) process-oriented culture.

Just Say Yes

Instead of picking sides and pursuing only one goal (A or B), wisdom teaches us that leaders at XYZ and EC should have worked together to manage the tension between the EC's small group culture (A) and XYZ's larger group culture (B). Instead of asking, *How do I achieve MY goal?* both sides should have brainstormed answers to the paradoxical question: *How might we stretch to achieve BOTH goals?*

I grew up in a small city in Connecticut. Like many cities, distinct parts of our town had their own unique neighborhood. There were Polish, Puerto Rican, Jewish, and Black sections of our town. To my young eyes, everyone seemed to work *with* each other during the day. Parents worked with coworkers while kids went to school with each other. At night everyone went home, where they often honored their cultural heritage with food, language, stories, and rituals. Each culture contributed to our town's culture. It was as if each group brought their unique dish to our town picnic.

Our town was not Mayberry, a perfect place where we all sang songs of unity. As I got older, I saw more racial and ethnic strife. Yet overall, the town seemed to manage the tension between our diversity (parts) and our community (whole) well.

« *The sun shines unity
so nature blooms diversity.* »

Patriot or Nationalist?

A buffet of unique cultures, contributing to a collective, is the heart of America's exceptionalism. Most countries were founded on common geography, religion, or ethnicity. The United States was founded more on differences than commonalities. Our ancestors came from somewhere else (*if* you trace America's history back far enough). America is a nation of immigrants. What made us great in days gone by has been our ability, over time, to manage the tension between our many nationalities and our one nation. We didn't do it well at first. We still struggle to embrace immigrants. But in time, our country's culture tends to build bridges that stretch between different ethnicities (parts) *and* a collective community (whole) based on shared values. Keeping us from being great these days is the notion that either side (our unique cultures *or* our country as a whole) is the right side. Nowhere is this mistake seen more plainly than when people confuse nationalism for patriotism.

Nationalists proclaim their nation's culture is superior and must either absorb smaller cultures (i.e., immigrants) or reject them completely. Patriots applaud their country's culture, but they also believe they should accommodate cultural diversity. Nationalists remind me of the Borg in *Star Trek*, hell-bent on dominating the universe. Patriots believe in the Federation—an organization that celebrates individuality and unity. The ability to integrate other cultures *at their own pace* (usually within a generation or two) is one of the keys to an exceptional country.

The wisdom of sages spoken through the ages teaches us that *divided,* we can still stand together *united.* Aristotle spoke of the *"Golden mean between the extreme."* Physicist Niels Bohr said, *"How wonderful that we have met with a paradox. Now we have some hope of making progress."* And historian/philosopher Huston Smith proclaimed, *"We must not let our differences blind us to the unity that binds us."* These wise souls encourage us to be Both/And thinkers in today's Either/Or culture. The older I get, the grayer things seem.

« *A true patriot salutes individual liberty
and embraces community responsibility.* »

Can You See the Me in We?

When the people lead, the leaders must follow. So, let's not be fooled by the false narrative of us versus them. That's propaganda promoted by people who profit by selling fear. They focus only on their parts OR the whole. Instead, let's stretch to embrace both our country's diversity and our commonality. Let's celebrate our many cultures and salute one nation under God as we pursue life, liberty, and happiness. Each of us can be lights of liberty, shining on bridges we build between the ME and WE.

« *The test of a first-rate intelligence
is the ability to hold two opposed ideas
in the mind at the same time,
and still retain the ability to function.* »

F. SCOTT FITZGERALD

I'm a Both/And Man in Either/Or Land

I'm a both/and man in either/or land
I'm a both/and man in either/or land
I'm doing what I can, trying to understand
Now you think in black or white
When gray matters were just, right?
I'm a both/and man in either/or land

We roamed cross country, like streams flowing free
We roamed cross country, like streams flowing free
With open eyes we could see, each branch made the tree
Our land's blooming tapestry
Each state part of one whole scene
We were both/and teens spreading our wings

When I flew away, don't know why you stayed
When I flew away, so sad you stayed
Where one-party-song played, broken records all day
That fertile mind of your youth
Trampled by those deaf to truth
Lost my both/and man to either/or land

You lost your way, wandered astray
Marched with a few who had tunnel views
Find your way back, please take the middle path
'Cause if you believe in Adam and Eve
Or if you're in sync with how Darwin thinks
You cannot deny, we're all one tribe

Once we were teens, living that golden mean
We spread wings way back then, we can all soar again
Our Both/And way, is stretch to think gray

Now we're the both/and band in either/or land
Now we're the both/and band in either/or land
Our reach extends, Left and Right need two hands
We think less black or white
Gray matters are just right
We're the both/and band in either/or land

We're a rubber band, stretching where we can
Love demands, we understand
God commands, we all expand…
In either/or land

Join the both/and band, In either/or land

CHAPTER 6

Do You Have Emotions OR Do They Have You?

Beach Blanket Outburst

Imagine you and a few friends are sitting on blankets at the beach, chatting about nothing. The hot sun bakes sunscreen on your backs, lovers stroll hand in hand, and children repair castles pounded by crashing waves. About twenty yards away from you, teenagers are playing volleyball. On several occasions, a player spikes the ball so hard that it rolls close to you and your friends. Each time, you get up, grab the ball, and toss it back to the players. But at no time do any of these kids acknowledge your gesture. No smile, nod, or grunt of appreciation. Nothing.

As the ball rolls close to your blanket one last time, you snap, "What the #%U$^$^%$ is wrong with you? Don't you have any *&!@^*& manners? Next time your ball comes near our blanket, I'm kicking it into the *&!@^*& ocean!"

Your stunned friends sit in embarrassed silence as one of the teenagers walks near to you, picks up his ball, stares at you with a wrinkled brow, shakes his head, and marches back to his game without saying a word.

Although this true story happened thirty-six years ago, I still wince at my lack of self-control. Yes, I lost my cool on that hot summer day. I'm not sure why I was so emotional about something so small. Maybe it was my immaturity, my need to be appreciated, or my attachment to good ole fashion manners. Regardless of what set me off, it was clear for all the beachgoers within earshot that I didn't have emotions that day; they had me. *When do your emotions have you?*

Before you answer that question, let's define emotional intelligence (EI) as *the ability to process emotions in a way that helps us think*. That definition leads us to ask this wise question when stressed: *How can I use my emotions to help me achieve my goal?* Had I asked this question on the beach, I might have paused, acknowledged my increasing irritation, and simply asked for what I wanted: "Hey guys, how about a thank-you once in a while?"

Emotions flow from our brain's limbic system (amygdala), sometimes referred to as our reptilian brain. This is where our feelings and fight-or-flight mechanisms live. When we are stressed, our reptilian brain takes over because it "thinks" the best way to survive at that moment is to fight or take flight. Thus, it shuts down our analytical neocortex—the rational, thinking part of our brain. No wonder it's so hard to think clearly under pressure (or on the beach if you're irritated by teenagers playing volleyball).

The Case of the Happy CEO

Several years ago, a CEO named Mark invited me to meet with him to discuss the progress of his executive, Pat. Mark began our meeting by declaring that Pat was "a different person" because of her dramatic growth in her leadership skills. Mark pointed out that organizations couldn't grow unless people did. He was delighted that Pat was growing so much, especially when stressed.

I told the CEO that I had recruited a few of Pat's peers and direct reports to be part of our coaching process (with Pat's approval). These internal advocates supplied timely, frequent, and accurate feedback to Pat. This, combined with the weekly coaching sessions she had with me, helped Pat rein in her emotions. She was managing her emotions instead of having them manage her.

Strike When the Iron Is COLD

Next time you feel your temperature rising, count to ten, and answer these five questions:

1. *What am I feeling?*

2. *What does it make me want to do?*

3. *What will happen (short and long term) if I do that?*

4. *What outcomes (short and long term) do I really want?*

5. *Who can help me brainstorm options to achieve my outcomes?*

Carry these questions with you. Share them with friends. Discuss them with colleagues. Science says had I paused to answer these questions at the beach thirty-six years ago, I *probably* would not have allowed my emotions to get the better of me. And as we will discuss in the next chapter, the essence of science is prediction.

« Reacting in anger or annoyance will not advance one's ability to persuade. »

RUTH BADER GINSBURG

CHAPTER 7

The Essence of Science Is Prediction

It's the kind of conversation you never want to have. Yet 2.1 million people do have a variation of this conversation every year. In winter of 1998, my straight-shooting brother Tom called to tell me, "Dave, Mom has lung cancer." I don't recall the rest of the call. I do remember discussing where she was going to be treated. We wanted to make sure Mom received the best care possible.

Think about that. What does it really mean to "receive the best care"? For me, a researcher with considerable healthcare experience, it entailed making sure Mom received the care that would give her the greatest chance of surviving this devastating disease. I wanted her to go where caregivers knew what therapies worked best. I wanted a team of healthcare experts to take care of my Mom.

Just Say Know to the Experts

It's popular these days to doubt the experts. Some media pundits even deny the fact that there are facts. To which I say yes, a healthy skepticism is often called for. But to deny all facts and all experts is unwise. Next time a denier tells you they don't believe in experts, ask them who they want to treat their loved ones when they become ill.

So, how do we know if someone is truly an expert? The dictionary defines an expert as one who *"has a comprehensive and authoritative knowledge in a particular area."* Experts use their vast knowledge and experience to achieve predictable outcomes. They help us understand which choices probably lead to which outcomes. In medicine, we rely on healthcare experts to give patients the greatest odds of beating a disease. At high-end restaurants, we want expert chefs to provide predictable, delicious dinners. When we drive, we rely on expert engineers to maintain the traffic lights to keep us moving safely.

Experts acquire and maintain their authoritative knowledge in two ways. First, they learn from others. They stay abreast of the latest developments by reading scientific journals/books, talking with expert colleagues, and attending educational conferences and workshops.

The second way experts gain and sustain their knowledge is by learning from personal experience. They learn by doing in environments that provide quantity and quality feedback. Consider oncologists who diagnose, treat, and monitor lung cancer patients every day. They acquire excellent experience. Family doctors who practice in rural hospitals may see only a few cancer patients a year. This limits their experiential learning.

My Addiction to Prediction

To summarize, experts integrate the latest knowledge with their experience to provide the best odds for success. Thus, the essence of science is seldom certainty; it is prediction. There are no guarantees. Medical researchers use the tools and rules of science to improve the chances that patients recover. Our family wanted Mom to have the treatment that provided the greatest probability of surviving lung cancer. We decided to have her treated by the experts at Yale hospital in New Haven, CT, several miles from her home.

By now, you may realize that this chapter is less about where my Mom was treated and more about how to assess expertise. Most experts contend that if we follow their advice (i.e., suggestions, recommendations, instructions, directions, plans, prescriptions), we will achieve our desired outcome. Thus, their advice is actually a prediction. They claim if we do what they say, we will get what we want.

Should we believe what they say because they are celebrities, have millions of followers, or shout through a megaphone? No, No, No. We should recall our definition of an expert and only listen to those who have *comprehensive and authoritative knowledge*.

Here's the Beef

Next time someone offers you advice by claiming, *"If you do this... you will achieve that...,"* ask them, *"How do you know that?"* Their response will often tell you whether they possess the knowledge and experience that predicts success or not. *"How do you know that?"* helps distinguish true experts from false prophets because it invites a dialogue about the basis of their assertion. Experts are delighted to discuss the evidence behind their suggestions. Fake prophets become defensive when asked to show proof that backs up their claim. No wonder Plato pointed out, "An empty vessel makes the loudest sound."

I encourage you to ask yourself (and others) throughout your day, *"How do I (you) know that?"* Consider also asking this question when you:

1. Watch TV pundits make bold statements (e.g., *America has interfered in eighty-one foreign elections since World War II*).

2. Read editorials offering prescriptions (e.g., *this healthcare plan lowers your costs*).

3. Hear political elites pontificate on trade (e.g., *trade wars caused the Great Depression*).

4. Discuss politics (e. g., *a gun at home increases the risk of homicide for women by 500%*).

Our family applied the wisdom of this chapter to give Mom the best chance of curing her cancer. We felt the Yale experts offered her the best odds. Unfortunately, they were not Gods. Mom died six months after my brother's call. There's a hole in my heart where she used to be. I still miss her terribly. But I never miss the opportunity to help others understand that science is a process for gaining knowledge. It has the tools and rules to help us make predictions based on evidence.

> « *There are in fact two things,*
> *science and opinion.*
> *The former begets knowledge,*
> *the latter ignorance.* »
>
> HIPPOCRATES

CHAPTER 8

Vision Without Feedback Is Tunnel Vision

You're sitting on a bench, watching a woman under attack by a man covered by protective padding. Her "assailant" looks like a baseball catcher and police-dog trainer rolled into one. After several women, one at a time, beat the crap out of their attacker, you notice that each woman scans the gymnasium, then sprints off the wrestling mat.

Tears moistened my eyes as I joined the crowd applauding all these women for graduating from their eight-week self-defense class. After the ceremony, I asked the instructor why every woman paused after defeating her predator and took a few precious seconds to look around *before* running to "safety." She explained that assault victims can become so laser-focused on the danger in front of them that they miss harm coming from behind them. Stress can cause tunnel vision.

The Trouble with Town Hall Meetings

Consider the case of a senior executive, Alan, who was upset that his firm's recent attempt to reorganize was going poorly. When I asked if his executive team communicated a vision of where they wanted the organization to go and why, he snapped, "Of course, Dave."

I pressed on, "How is your executive team getting quality feedback from employees?"

"We are having more town hall meetings," he pushed back.

Alan and I then had a frank discussion about the limits of town hall meetings. I pointed out that although town hall meetings are fine for broadcasting the news, they rarely obtain the candid feedback needed to course correct. Employees often see those meetings as choreographed dog-and-pony shows. They seldom foster open, honest dialogue about the progress or problems of major initiatives. Alan then admitted that he and his executive team had become narrow-minded by thinking town hall meetings could furnish all the feedback they needed. They are now supplementing their town hall meetings by cascading messages through supervisors and conducting anonymous employee surveys.

« *Leaders with vision must help*
others see tomorrow...today. »

Can You Handle the Truth?

On a more personal note, many years ago, I asked my close friend Mack to give me feedback on a critical new product I was developing. It was to be the foundation for my new business. Mack told me he didn't think it had any chance of success. I was hurt by what I felt was his lack of support, but it turned out he was spot on. My vision became tunnel vision. I lost a lot of money on that venture because I failed to heed Mack's course-correcting feedback. It was a costly way to learn this wise lesson: loyalty to the truth is the foundation upon which loyalty to people must rest. If people can't handle the truth, that's their problem.

When does your vision become tunnel vision? How will you solicit feedback to remove your blind spots? Do you remind those around you that loyalty to the truth is the precursor to loyalty to the person?

The self-defense class, Alan's coaching, and Mack's candid comments remind us that we all have blinders, especially when stressed. Of course, big-picture goals and dreams are critical to achievement. But as you march boldly in the direction of your dreams, recall Ben Franklin's wise warning: "A man in passion rides a mad horse."

> « We must not let what may be possible
> keep us from what is probable. »

Soliciting external and internal feedback keeps us from flying, like Icarus, too close to the sun. Inviting external feedback from truth-telling friends, like Mack, is a fantastic way to "keep it real." Don't let an inflated ego or deflated self-esteem cause you to seek counsel only from those who pat you on the back when you really need a kick in the ass.

Internal feedback is the second way to stay on track. It has two components:

Self-talk. What do you say to yourself when you stray off course or smack into obstacles? Does your self-talk lift you up or hold you down? I encourage you to cultivate a growth mindset, one that lifts you up when you're down. Our minister suggests we ask this energy-directing question: *Where's the blessing in the messing?*

Inner wisdom. Years ago, my boss marched into my office and growled, "Dave, just once, I would like to come into your office and see you thinking more and doing less." How about you? Are you so immersed in outside noise (e-mail, texting, selfies, Instagram, Facebook…) that you drown out the feedback from your own, still, small voice? For the last thirty years, my favorite technique to hear my inner wisdom has been to write "morning pages"—three pages of nonstop writing, as defined by Julia Cameron in her wonderful book *The Artist's Way*. Morning pages are three pages of writing whatever comes to mind. You don't think, ponder, or contemplate. You just keep your hand moving and let what comes to mind splat onto the paper. This is how I discovered the lyrics in this book. Give it a shot. I think you'll find it a useful way to hear your internal wisdom and creativity…without a boss growling at you.

Follow the wisdom in this chapter as you pursue your vision, dreams, and goals. But don't let your vision become tunnel vision, as I did with my high-priced product that flopped. Your truth-telling friends and your inner wisdom are the dynamic duo that can keep you from being blinded by the light you seek. These external and internal voices can help you hear the wisdom in feedback that will keep you on track.

CHAPTER 9

If Everything Is Important, Nothing Is Strategic

The company president, Marcia, looked up from the reports scattered across her cluttered desk. "Come in, Dave. I know that you only come to see me with important leadership issues. So, what's up?"

I replied the way she wanted to hear it—bluntly. "Marcia, many of your senior and mid-level leaders feel buried by the numerous huge projects they are working on. I think you need to help them prioritize these initiatives, so they can focus on those that are most important."

"They are all important!" she barked.

I barked back, "If everything is important, nothing is strategic."

One Whale Is Worth a Thousand Minnows

I wish I could tell you this story ended well. It didn't. Neither coaching, consulting, nor counseling Marcia's executive team slowed this train-wreck of leadership malpractice. Marcia neither prioritized nor decreased the deluge of projects drowning her team. Within a year, more than half of them resigned or retired.

To be strategic is difficult because it demands we say no to many good ideas to focus on a few excellent ideas. Former Apple president Steve Jobs summed it up wisely: "I'm as proud of what we didn't do as I am of what we did do. It comes from saying no to 1,000 things to make sure we don't get on the wrong track or try to do too much."

I was an average salesperson for the first couple of years until I read *Strategic Selling*, which taught me how to identify my "best customers" and pursue only those prospects with similar profiles as my best customers. I became a top salesperson because I had learned to be a focused laser instead of a scattered shotgun.

Less Is More

To sell strategically is a practical application of the "Pareto principle," named after the Italian economist Vilfredo Pareto, who observed that 80% of the land was owned by 20% of the people. More broadly, the Pareto principle says that *approximately* 20% of the causes create *about* 80% of the effect. Here are ten examples:

✔ 20% of the customers create 80% of the sales.

✔ 20% of the apps on our phones are used 80% of the time.

✔ 20% of our contacts are responsible for 80% of our phone calls.

✔ 20% of the meeting agenda yields 80% of results.

✔ 20% of our activities produce 80% of our joy.

✔ 20% of the tasks (on our "To Do" list) produce 80% of the results.

✔ 20% of the job requirements constitute 80% of the job.

✔ 20% of the people cause 80% of the problems.

✔ 20% of Twitter users create 80% of the tweets.

✔ The top 20% of earners pay more than 80% of the US taxes.

Unlike Steve Jobs, Marcia allowed the meaningless many to mask the fundamental few. She confused activity for accomplishment. She fished for minnows while standing on whales. Steve Jobs knew he didn't have enough time to do everything, so he focused on a few strategic things. That's how he revolutionized four industries: computers, music, movies, and phones with the Macintosh, iTunes, Pixar, and the iPhone.

How about you? Are you like Marcia, a scattered person who chases every shining target? Or will you follow Steve's lead by focusing on the few that mean the most to you? Put the wisdom of the Pareto principle to work for you by answering a great time management question throughout your day: "Where will I get the biggest bang for my buck?"

« *To attain knowledge, add things every day.*
To attain wisdom, remove things every day. »

LAO TZU

We Move in the Direction of the Pictures We Place, or Let Others Place, in Our Minds

Don't think of a red rose. Don't think of a red rose. Don't think of a red rose. Okay, what just popped into your head? A red rose?

How Does Your Garden Grow?

This simple visualization exercise introduces us to the powerful role pictures play in our brains. Neuroscientists report that about 50% of the brain is dedicated to vision-related tasks. Think of the brain like it's a garden. A garden grows whatever is planted. It doesn't care what we plant. It's neutral. Whether they be seeds or weeds, our minds' fertile soil will sow what is planted. If we plant nothing, weeds will grow. Why? Because the winds of negativity are always blowing, *and* the brain is always on the lookout for danger. That's how weeds grow.

What You See Is What You Get

My family gave me a nickname after I grew my beard—Moses. For many years, the picture I had of myself was that of a sage serving words of wisdom to hungry audiences. But as my self-awareness grew, it became clear that my Moses persona was just feeding my bloated ego. So, I pulled those weeds and planted a new, positive picture in my brain. This picture evolved into my goal of being a coach, educator, and consultant who offered a buffet of tools to those who came to the table. My new "selfie" felt less self-serving because it focused on serving others.

When we set goals, we increase success because goals plant positive pictures in our brains, thereby focusing our time and energy. That's why it's wise to set SMART (Specific, Measurable, Attainable, Responsible, Timed) goals. They don't guarantee achievement, but they do increase the odds.

I recommend you write short-term and long-term goals. As you write them, identify a few of the challenges you might encounter and how you will overcome them. Conclude your SMART goal-setting session by brainstorming the words that describe how you will look and feel achieving your goals (e.g., proud, confident, joyful, successful, disciplined, first-rate).

« Always be a first-rate version of yourself,
instead of a second-rate version of someone else. »

JUDY GARLAND

Review your goals every day and nurture the positive picture you have of yourself as you achieve them. How surprised will you be when you see the most important selfie is the picture you have of yourself in your brain?

CHAPTER 11

How Things Start Is Where Things Go

I promised to provide product information to a UCLA graduate student, Marvin, when I sold medical equipment for XYZ company many years ago. UCLA was one of my best customers, and I knew all the key decision-makers. Marvin was *not* one of them. Maybe that's why I dropped the ball. I don't remember. All I recall is that I didn't get him the information I promised.

A few years after my incident of forgetfulness, I was hired by UCLA, as was Marvin. On occasion, Marvin and I *should* have worked together on various projects, but we never did. He always avoided me. One day, I casually asked my boss if he had any idea why Marvin avoided me.

"He doesn't trust you." My boss explained that Marvin told him that I hadn't delivered on past promises when I worked for XYZ company. Yikes! I had forgotten all about my lack of follow-through years earlier. Marvin had not.

> « *The past does not equal the future,*
> *but it does predict it.* »

The story illustrates that *how things start is where they go*. It should serve as a reminder that what we decide to do or not do has consequences. Our actions ripple into the future, like stones thrown in a lake.

Nowhere is this more evident than how so many people start their day. They wake up and quickly reach for their cell phones, turn on social media, and start texting/e-mailing/tweeting. They allow these morning actions to become daily distractions. I suggest you avoid beginning your day that way. Instead, focus your attention on your intention.

> « *The first hour of the morning,*
> *is the rudder of the day.* »
>
> HENRY WARD BEECHER

Let Energy Flow Where Attention Goes

How the morning starts is where it's headed is important to understand because a thought in motion will stay in motion unless acted on by another thought (apologies to Sir Isaac Newton). You can put this principle to the test by conducting a three-minute experiment. Take these simple steps every day for one week:

1. Read a positive affirmation when you first wake up.

2. Write an intention for your day on a blank three-by-five index card. (Keep it with you all day.)

3. Repeat your intention to yourself every time you touch or see your index card.

« Sow a thought, you reap an action;
sow an action, you reap a habit;
sow a habit, you reap a character;
sow a character, you reap a destiny. »

RALPH WALDO EMERSON

Adapt these steps to start your day and help you stay focused all day. Perhaps I may have had a better relationship with Marvin at UCLA if I knew this when I was at XYZ.

CHAPTER 12

Experimentation Is the Mother of Innovation

"Ray, this software is fantastic. It's just what my customers are asking for. They're going to love it." I could hardly contain my enthusiasm for Ray's new software.

A few days after my conversation with Ray, I showed the new software to Dr. Laguna in his hospital office. Dr. Laguna was a wise old soul and a skeptical cardiologist. As I concluded the demo, I expected to hear his thoughtful and challenging questions. Instead, he sang the tune every salesperson loves to hear near the end of a long sales process.

"Okay, Dave, I'll buy your computer network, but only because your new software is a sign that your company is finally learning to be more innovative. I don't want to get stuck with software that's obsolete in two years."

A Closed Mind Is a Wonderful Thing to Lose

Much to my disappointment, Ray quit six months later. His hotshot development team was disbanded. When I saw Ray at a subsequent medical conference, he explained that he left our company because he grew tired of arguing with closed-minded engineers. He lamented that the research and development (R&D) group suffered from the "not invented here" (NIH) syndrome. If R&D didn't create it, they wouldn't support it.

Dr. Laguna was right to be concerned about our company's inability to innovate. Their bureaucratic culture and burdensome R&D process crushed Ray's experimental mindset. Our US sales continued their downward spiral after Ray's departure. I accepted a leadership position at UCLA, and our division was absorbed into a larger division within the company.

There Is No Failure, Only Feedback

Organizations, large and small, eventually die if they don't practice the wisdom in this chapter—*experimentation is the mother of innovation.* This applies today more than ever because our world is increasingly Volatile, Uncertain, Complex, Ambiguous, and Paradoxical (VUCAP). Employees *at all levels* must be engaged in the innovation process by developing the experimental mindset if the organization is to succeed in this whitewater work environment.

An experimental mindset asks, "How can we test this idea rapidly?" It applies to minor and major projects at home and work. For example, when I was at UCLA, I overheard a brief conversation between one of our administrators and a professor. The professor was wading his way through the twelve-page monthly budget report. The administrator later told me that she often needed to answer questions about the lengthy report. I asked her if she could help create a shorter and more "user-friendly" version. She and her supervisor proudly delivered a simple two-page summary a week later. Our faculty was delighted.

Experimental thinking reinforces a growth mindset, which says we don't fail when we fall if we learn. So, experiment with this approach by testing it in different areas of your life. At work, consider updating old policies and procedures. At home, try new restaurants, genres of movies and books, hobbies, social activities, volunteer groups. My all-time favorite comes from a colleague at Emory University who says to experiment, brush your teeth with the opposite hand.

CHAPTER 13

History Is Trajectory, Not Destiny

Sally's father shoved her out of their thatched hut into the dark, damp forest to gather mushrooms for dinner. Her mother stood in the doorway and sighed, too tired to defend her little girl this time. Mom forced a weak smile and a half-hearted wave goodbye as Sally disappeared into the late-afternoon shadows. Mom shuffled back into the dingy hut, shoulders slumped.

As the sun sank, Sally searched for the elusive mushrooms hiding among the moss-covered ground. Sadly, on this day, she wandered too far from home and too close to the forbidden cave. As she was about to head back home, she heard a faint cry from inside the cave. Lured by the weak weeping and the impulse to nourish her nature, Sally crept closer to the cave entrance. She leaned forward, straining to hear cries. Her neck stretched like a turtle. One more step closer…SNAP…she stepped on a dry twig and froze. Instantly, a big, bloody lobster-like claw lunged out of the cave toward Sally's slender waist.…

STOP!!! Stop the story right there! About thirty years ago, I told this story while my eight-year-old niece Sami, my mom, and I drove home after visiting my sister. Sami and I told the story together, tag-team style. I would tell the story for a minute, then Sami would take over for a minute, then back to me. We went back and forth like this for the entire forty-five-minute drive home. When we pulled into Mom's driveway, Sami tied a bow around our story: "And they lived happily ever after."

"That was a delightful story," Mom gushed. "Where did it come from? How did you both know it so well?"

Sami and I looked at each other and burst out laughing. Sami exclaimed, "Nana, we just made it up as we went along. We never told this story before."

Your Hero's Journey

Most fairytales and adventure stories begin with the central character (the hero, heroine, or protagonist) in their homeland engaged in their day-to-day activities. (Think of the opening scenes of *Cinderella, Wonder Woman, Game of Thrones, The Wizard of Oz.*) One day, our heroine is called, tricked, or seduced into new, dangerous lands. Thus begins the grand adventure, full of lions, and tigers, and bears. Our heroine must overcome these daunting challenges, often with the help of a friendly wizard, dragon, or knight. Eventually, she sees her light and conquers the night.

In fairytales, things seldom get better until our heroine or hero grows. The great irony is that overcoming the journey's obstacles often builds the strength they need to conquer their foe, discover the treasure, and find their way home. They share their life-transforming insights with their village. Everybody celebrates, like at the end of a *Shrek* movie. And they all live happily ever after....

What's Your Story?

I told many made-up-on-the-spot stories with my nieces and nephews over the years, usually with some lesson or moral beneath the surface. One of the lessons I try to infuse in many of these stories is that **history is not destiny, but it is trajectory.** As we drove home that day, I steered the story Sami and I told in this direction because I wanted Sami to see that her past need not dictate her future. The heroine in our story overcame her difficult history and lived happily ever after. Things got better because she grew bigger. You can grow too…if you listen to Sir Isaac Newton.

If you recall, Newton's first law of motion states that *an object in motion stays in motion in the same direction unless acted upon by another force.* This law teaches us that when we want to change the direction of our lives, to overcome our history, we need to tell stories that answer four powerful questions:

1. Where am I going?

2. Why is this journey important?

3. Who can show me the way?

4. How will I turn obstacles into stepping-stones?

Stronger in Broken Places

The challenges we encounter on our journey can make us or break us. We choose which. In many stories, including mine, the protagonists choose to use the resistance they face to gain strength. Climbing today's hill strengthens their will to conquer tomorrow's mountain. Our challenges can do the same for us.

« *There's what happened, and then…
there's our story about what happened.* »

It's wise to tell stories that transcend our history so we may manifest our destiny. It's wiser still to listen to what our stories tell us.

CHAPTER 14

Beliefs Are the Periscopes of Life

Two college friends suddenly grabbed my arms and dragged me off the barstool. A third yelled, "Come on, Dave, stop bothering that old guy; you've had too much to drink. Let's go!"

I sighed, shook my head, and thought, *Here we go again. If I fight their vice grip, it looks like I'm drunk. If I let them drag me out of this bar, it looks like I'm drunk. Either way, everybody in this bar will think I'm drunk.* Forty-five years later, my friends (yes, we are all still friends) and I laugh about it. At a deeper level, it took me a long time to figure out that dragging me out of the bar was revealing a rigid belief that was a blind spot for me.

My Double-Edged Sword

I had strong convictions in my younger days. My single-mindedness helped me succeed in some areas of my life. But at times, my convictions descended into stubbornness. That's what dragging me out of the bar was all about. I had this strong belief that if I talked to old men in bars, I could glean words of wisdom about life. Not a bad idea for my first "research project," right? Yes, BUT not a great idea when you overdo it and your friends start shouting, "Enough, let's go, Dave!"

Any strength carried too far can become a weakness—a double-edged sword. I was so focused on "interviewing" these old men that I couldn't see that I was frustrating my friends. I realize now that my rigidity flowed from my insecurity. (Only the insecure act so sure of themselves.) Somewhere deep inside, I clung to the belief that my value was tied to my accomplishments. This was a side-effect of growing up in a large family where Mom had little time for kids and Dad gave too much time to beer. My rigid beliefs in college were whispers of that little boy seeking approval and a connection to a father figure. William Wordsworth was wise when he pointed out, "The child is the father of the man."

Seeing Is Not Believing; Believing Is Seeing

Striving to achieve difficult goals has been a blessing and curse throughout my life. On the one hand, my strong belief in achievement helped me accomplish many goals. Yet, this belief has also contributed to my narrow-mindedness at times. Periscopes, like beliefs, can fixate attention in one direction. But they can also offer a wide perspective if we rotate them to scan the horizon. That's why *beliefs are the periscopes of life.* Here are three overlapping ideas that can help rotate our periscopes.

1. The loyal opposition

Social philosopher Eric Hoffer points out that "it's easier to love humanity than to like our neighbors." Perhaps that's why we are commanded to love our neighbors as ourselves. One way to show love is to invite those close to us to share their beliefs. Family, friends, and neighbors should feel at home sharing different views. A wise mentor once told me that it's useful to ask the "loyal opposition" what they see. Their contrasting views can help us see old landscapes with new eyes. We don't need to agree with what they say about what they see. But it is wise for us to listen to their view as we rotate the periscope together.

2. A half-truth is a whole lie

Two blindfolded men touch an elephant. One touches the tail and declares elephants are long and thin. The other feels the tusk and asserts that elephants are smooth and hard. Each experience is true, yet each conclusion is false…because, as the old Yiddish saying goes, a half-truth is a whole lie.

The elephant story also introduces us to the confirmation bias: a decision-making trap that occurs when we favor information that confirms our beliefs. If we are in touch only with the news that supports our biased views or connect only with like-minded friends on social media, our conclusions are often false…because their half-truths are whole lies.

Of course, it's fine to describe our experience when we touch an elephant while wearing a blindfold. But it's unwise to conclude that what we feel is the whole truth. Our experience is true, but our conclusion is often false. To draw a truthful conclusion, we must remove our blindfolds. That's what I did.

Several years ago, I discovered that some of the news I was taking in was from biased sources. I decided I needed to remove my own blindfold. Thus began a search for news sources that would tell me the whole, inconvenient truth. I discovered *The Economist* magazine, *USA Today* newspaper, and *The BBC* television offered fact-based news and balanced views that could help me see objectively. How can you be more open to see the elephant's majestic beauty?

3. The question that elevates the conversation

The third periscope principle reminds us to surround ourselves with friends and colleagues who pledge allegiance to the truth, the whole truth, and nothing but the truth...because *our opinions don't set us free; the truth does.*

When someone shares their opinion, we want those around us to ask the question that elevates the conversation. It's the same question that helps discern the expert from the charlatan. Spend time with those bold enough to ask and answer, *How do you know that?*

> « *Speaking truth to power*
> *begins with the truth.* »

Not long ago, a friend asked me how I had become more flexible as I got older. I explained that it took years for me to learn how to apply these three principles of belief. I confessed I still get stuck at times. I thanked him for being one of my lifelong friends who has the courage and wisdom to tell me the whole truth...and the strength to drag me off the barstool when my periscope gets stuck.

A Half-Truth Is a Whole Lie

Lonely streets,
Empty factories all around
Ghosts adrift, broken parking lots,
Beached moorings in our towns.
Fields overgrown, dead-end streets,
Echo silence day and night.
Fading memories replay,

Where vivid dreams took flight.
Feel our father's whisper,
Glimpse tears in shattered glass.
Can wounded places heal?
Will we find our way back?

> *A half-truth is a whole lie,*
> *Do we really hear from both sides?*
> *A half-truth is a whole lie,*
> *Do we see how closed minds divide?*

Drove to the factory,
Crossed enraged picket lines.
A stunned son of sixteen,
I couldn't read the signs.
Dad parked somewhere out back,
We felt safe now from attack.
"Was that your friend Jack
Who kicked our car?" I asked.
He sighed, "Managers get stuck
Between different points of view.
But life's not black OR white,
One-sided stories aren't all true."

> *A half-truth is a whole lie,*
> *Do we really hear from both sides?*
> *A half-truth is a whole lie,*
> *Do we see how closed minds divide?*

So many factories,
Fallen bricks now gather dust.
All those futures canceled
Blinded by broken trust,
Dad lost it all, slid into hell
A deep, dark depression,
Shuffled round our house,
Lost in his own recession.
One summer day, I wasn't home,
To see him grab that knife.
Dad tore a hole in my soul,
The day the night took his light.

Lessons of hope can spring
From the pain of winter's past.
History is not destiny,
When scars blaze new paths.
We've climbed so many mountains,
Gazed at fog's veil from above.
Hear our fathers' prayer,
For town n country loved…

A half-truth is a whole lie,
But listening is uniting for both sides.
A half-truth is a whole lie,
Hear how open minds bridge divides.

Nations die by suicide too,
Papercuts every day.
So, tune out biased media,
Prevent truth's decay.
Lower your own drawbridge,
Invite outsiders in.
It takes each village, loving thy neighbors,
To make us all great again.
We the people now proclaim,
Our wounded places heal,
Differences don't blind us
To the unity that binds us,
As the whole truth reveals.

CHAPTER 15

The Meaning of Life Is the Meaning We Give Its Moments

Mike and I decided to climb one more long, steep mountain road on the last morning of our cycling trip. Although we had never climbed this one before, we had cycled side-by-side up hundreds of winding roads over the previous thirty years. We soon fell into our slow, steady rhythm as we ascended into the mountain's morning fog.

Without warning, Mike suddenly rose out of his saddle and blasted off like a rocket, leaving me behind. I tried to peddle faster, but my tired legs said no. Mike faded into the mist ahead. I took a deep breath and resigned myself to bike up this mountain alone. My mind drifted. *I wonder what got into him. We bike alongside each other for days, and now he takes off like a mountain goat? Oh well, he'll wait for me at the top. I just need to keep plugging along.*

About twenty minutes later, I finally reached the top. There was my buddy, straddling his bike and sipping from his silver water bottle. "Boy, Mike, you really took off like a shot," I panted, wiping the sweat from my eyes.

"That's because I'm a sprinter and you're a plugger! Come on, let's head home." He mounted his bike and began coasting down the other side of the mountain.

My stomach tightened and my brow wrinkled as I tried to make sense of what he just said: *A plugger? A plugger is a slowpoke—like a turtle! Did my best friend just disrespect me? What's up with that?* My mind swirled in silence all the way home.

What do you think? Did Mike insult me by calling me a plugger? When I ask participants in my workshops, about half of them say YES, the other half say NO; I was not insulted. The honest answer is yes and no, because my thinking makes them so. If I chose to think about it negatively, then I was disrespected. If I decided to interpret it as a simple observation by a great friend, I was not dissed.

This simple story serves as a reminder that accessing free will is a wonderful way to climb our own mountains. It's also how Dr. Viktor Frankl survived his horrifying climb.

Trauma Is a Given, Drama Is a Choice

Dr. Viktor Frankl was a psychiatrist whose pregnant wife, parents, and brother were all murdered in the Holocaust. He spent three agonizing years in concentration camps, and upon his release, he authored an illuminating book. *In Man's Search for Meaning*, he wrote:

Everything can be taken from a person but one thing: the last of the human freedoms—to choose one's attitude in any given set of circumstances, to choose one's own way...every day, every hour....

Dr. Frankl taught the importance of accessing our freedom to make meaning out of what happens to us. He was a victim of incredible horror, yet he refused to play the role of victim. Let me make this clear: No reasonable person can doubt that he, *and six million Jews*, were victims of horrible atrocities during World War II. Having survived this savage brutality, Dr. Frankl then spent the rest of his life teaching people to make meaning out of whatever they experienced. He believed that trauma was a given, but drama was an option. (Having said that, we must also recognize that many people need and should receive professional help to manage their trauma.)

> « *Freedom is what you do*
> *with what's been done to you.* »
>
> JEAN-PAUL SARTRE

Lightning Striking Again

Life is an accumulation of years. Those years consist of months, which are made of days consisting of hours, which are composed of minutes. Thus, life is an accumulation of minutes (525,600 minutes per year x 85 years = 44,676,000 minutes in an average life span). These minutes of life are like grains of sand slipping through the hourglass of life. The sand represents our experiences as they slide into the past.

Some of our difficult experiences may feel random. They are uninvited, unpredictable, and unwelcome. Like bolts of lightning, they strike us down. We fall victim to circumstances in a flash. This is called "*sh*t happens.*" The question is not if we will get smacked down; rather, *how long will we choose to stay there?*

> « *Suffering is the story*
> *I tell myself about my pain.* »

I don't believe we are 100% responsible for the winds of adversity that blow as we climb our mountains. I do think we are responsible for choosing how we think about what happens to us. Which is why, weeks after that mountain bike ride, I asked Mike why he called me a plugger. He explained that my bike's gears allowed me to spin more easily than his bigger gears allowed him to spin. My gears matched my cycling style—slow and steady. His higher gears dictated that he had to grind slowly to match my turtle-like pace. After cycling side-by-side for a few days, he was tired of peddling slowly. So on a whim, he decided to pick up his pace. That's why he took off. That's all there was to it. I had made up a stupid story in my head about being disrespected by my best friend. That's called making a mountain out of a molehill. Ugh.

This entire experience taught me that Mike is right; I am a plugger, both on and off the bike. In fact, I have been a slow, steady climber all my life. I just hadn't accepted it until this incident. Now, I'm proud to call myself a plugger. Mike and I are still best friends and cycle side-by-side, most of the time.

Are You a Meaning-Making Machine?

To live happily ever after, we need to be meaning-making machines. We must consciously choose how to think about what happens to us. Here's a simple but not always easy way to do just that.

Next time you have a difficult experience, feel free to moan and groan about it for a while, like I did after Mike called me a plugger. We are human beings that need to yelp when wounded. Then, tune into your inner wisdom. It will tell you when it's time to graduate from *What just happened?* to *What does this mean to me?* To help you make meaning out of it, brainstorm answers to three questions:

1. How can I QTIP—**Q**uit **T**aking **I**t **P**ersonally?

2. Where's my blessing here?

3. Who can help me process this?

Answer these questions to help you avoid making a mountain out of a molehill. Your answers may even remind you that you have known all along about the wisdom in this chapter. You've known ever since you heard the childhood rhyme, *Sticks and stones may break my bones, but words shall never hurt me.*

Can you see how happy you'll be when you stop playing that broken record of *Woe is me?* And choose to sing, **WOW, it's up to me!**

WOW, It's Up to Me

Climbing mountains side-by-side,
Swapping stories as we rise.
Ascending souls on untamed roads,
Friendship riding, trust uniting, truth be told.

So surprised that foggy morn,
One raced ahead with no warn.
I tried so hard to stay with him
But I fell back, alone I cracked, spun tales of suffering.
>   **WOE is me,**
>   **WOW, it's up to me.**
>   **Which one I choose is my reality**

At last, I reached the top,
Relieved my friend finally stopped.
You raced ahead, tell me WHY?
I'm a sprinter, you're a plugger, his cold reply.
>   **WOE is me,**
>   **WOW, it's up to me.**
>   **Which one I choose is my reality**

Down the mountain, mute the way.

Back home, I moaned to mates.

One winced; *WOE, you've been dissed!*

One laughed; *WOW, don't be pissed at THIS.*

Stunned receiving gave two meanings, WOW lit my clouds.

In receiving we make meaning, WOW thundered loud.

> **WOE or WOW is me,**
>
> **WOW's a choice, I see.**
>
> **WOW is now my reality**

Climbing mountains side-by-side,

Swapping stories as we rise.

Mountain echoes this they say

Tales are clay, shape fate today, choose WOW's way.

> **WOE or WOW is me,**
>
> **WOW's a choice, I see.**
>
> **WOW is now my reality**

WOW's destiny when mountains speak

CHAPTER 16

That Which Comes at You Is for You

Have you ever gazed upwards during tough times and wondered, "Why me?" That question is a variation of the one that has echoed through the centuries, "Why do bad things happen to good people?" I've pondered that question for over fifty years. I've read books, listened to preachers, talked with wise men and women, and old men in bars. This chapter is my answer to that question.

God's Test and Plan

Some believe that God is testing our faith when bad things happen to us, like Job in the Bible. Is God testing 5.6 million children around the world under the age of five who die every year from war, famine, or disease? I don't think so.

Others say that it's all part of God's plan for us. Is it part of God's plan to have 65 million refugees "live" in squalid camps all over the world? A refugee is "one who has been forced to flee their home by war or persecution." Imagine being forced to flee *your* home? What would it be like if bullets rained down on you and your family as you raced from your home to the nearest hospital for treatment and protection, only to have Syrian or Russian armies bomb that hospital? Is that all part of God's grand plan? I doubt it.

A Fatal Attraction

Some preachers proclaim that we attract everything that happens, good and bad, into our lives. This so-called secret is referred to as the "law of attraction." *There are no accidents* is their mantra. Does this explanation sound good when you ask, "Do you actually believe 6 million Jews attracted the horrendous atrocities of the Holocaust into their lives?" Do you think the 12.5 million slaves shipped across the seas invited this sin called slavery to spread across the globe? No way.

When bad things happen to good people, I don't think it's part of God's test or plan. Nor do I believe we are giant magnets attracting all our health, wealth, and sorrow to us.

> « I attribute my success to this:
> I never gave or took an excuse. »
>
> FLORENCE NIGHTINGALE

Gray May Be the Way

Understanding why bad things happen to good people begins by recognizing we have been asking a black-and-white question in a misguided attempt to answer a gray problem. Instead of asking *Why do bad things happen to good people?* we should ask this gray question: *How much am I contributing to what's happening to me?* We don't attract *everything* that happens to us, but we often attract some of it. Our answer places us on a grayscale—a continuum. On one end, we have no influence (0%) on what shows up in our lives (e.g., a plane crashes into your home). On the other end, we are completely (100%) responsible (e.g., we gain weight during the holidays). When something bad happens to us, a combination of randomness, thoughts, words, and deeds all conspire to place us somewhere on the grayscale of responsibility.

Consider people who smoke cigarettes. Researchers tell us that they are 15 to 30 times more likely to get lung cancer than non-smokers. They choose to inhale a toxic mix of 7,000 deadly chemicals into their lungs every time they light up. Did smoking cause my mom's cancer? Probably. Did it increase her odds she would get cancer? Definitely. Her actions place her on that grayscale, near the high responsibility side, alongside all my smoking aunts and uncles. Except for Aunt Viv, who never smoked and outlived them all. She died at the age of 94.

The Good, the Bad, or the Ugly

Of course, it's not always clear where we belong on that scale of responsibility. When the good, the bad, or the ugly come knocking on our door, it's hard to know what role we played in their arrival. Despite this ambiguity, we can still access our free will and choose how to think about what is coming at us. Like Dr. Viktor Frankl, we can make meaning out of difficult experiences. That's what I tried to do when my father committed suicide many years ago.

Dad's suicide was extremely painful. For months afterward, my brain spiraled down a dark hole of ruminating thoughts: *Why didn't I do more to help him? I should have seen it coming. If only I....* I sat in a swamp of self-pity for a long time. But over time, I began to realize that although I couldn't undo what Dad did, I could redo how I thought about it. I decided to *go* through the pain in order to *grow* from it. For me, this meant confronting two tough questions:

- *What role might I have played?*
- *How could what is before me...be for me?*

What Role Might I Have Played?

We each play a role in our family's dynamics. At an early age, I decided, subconsciously, my part was that of a peacemaker. I wanted our home to be friction-free, without conflict or drama. In case you haven't heard, friction-free living is not easy when there are five children, two parents (one alcoholic), and Gramma under one roof.

My peacemaker role surfaced when Dad dove into a deep depression after his factory closed. As my East Coast brothers and sister coped with this difficulty, I sat on the sidelines in California and let them make most of the decisions. I didn't want to cause any problems by pushing my opinion regarding Dad's treatment. To get along, I went along.

It took years for me to realize that I allowed my old role of peacemaker and my fear of friction or conflict to get in the way of discussing Dad's therapy options with my brothers and sister. I have no idea if my opinions would have made any difference. That's not the point here. The fact is, when adversity strikes, the first question to ask is: *What role might I have in this?* Answering this question well demands self-examination without self-flagellation. It asks us to put ourselves on the responsibility continuum without blaming ourselves. To know where we stand on the grayscale continuum is to begin making meaning out of our experience.

*« We had the experience
but missed the meaning. »*

T. S. ELIOT

What Is Before Me...Is for Me

Once we accept our role in a challenging experience, it's useful to see if there is something to learn from that experience. That leads to brainstorming answers to the second question: *How could what is before me...be for me?* Notice it's about what "could/might" be for us. There's seldom a clear answer here. It takes brainstorming to help find meaning. When I brainstormed answers to this question, I realized that although *Dad's suicide broke my heart, it didn't break me.* I was resilient.

I also concluded that I could mourn Dad's passing with tears, but I should also honor him with actions. I started to see my pain as a tool to scrape off the crusty barnacles that had protected my heart. I used the pain of my dad's death to open my heart and become more loving, gentle, forgiving, and kind (toward myself and others).

Next time you gaze upwards during tough times and wonder "Why me?" understand that the easy answer is usually wrong. The best we can do when life knocks us down is to stay down until we feel it's time to get up. We can then choose to think about our role and how we might grow through the experience, not merely go through it.

CHAPTER 17

Go Where You Need to Grow

I started my consulting and training business thirty years ago, confident that I could combine my research background, practical experience as a leader, and speaking skills into a booming boutique business empire. I discovered that it's easy to start a consulting practice but difficult to make money. I piled $50,000 of credit card debt on top of the $50,000 I had borrowed from family and friends in less than two years. Desperation filled my soul as I inched closer to losing my home.

One night, as I tossed and turned in bed with anxiety gnawing in the pit of my stomach, the still, small voice in my head said I needed to change my prayer from beseeching (begging for success) to surrendering (thy will be done). My new prayer went something like this, "Fine, Lord, take my home. It's been two years, and I have nothing but failed products and big bills to show for it. Just tell me what to do and where to go?" I went to sleep.

The next morning I awoke with an answer. Instead of straining to grow the product side of my business, I needed to develop the training side. Speaking/teaching was the real reason I started my business anyway. I decided that the fastest way to succeed was to contract with a seminar company.

Back in the 1990s, a seminar company was an organization that subcontracted a pool of speakers and trainers to teach specific topics. The seminar company would market to hundreds of local businesses that a specific subject would be taught at a given hotel on a particular date. The speaker/trainer (me) would show up to teach that topic all day and then move on to the next town that same night. Sounds great, right? Well, yes and no.

Yes, because the seminar company's marketing machine guaranteed a ready-made audience and plenty of speaking/teaching. No, because the pay was exceptionally low. So low, in fact, that I needed to teach every day, all day, often three weeks out of every month, just to pay my bills.

Hit the Road Jack

For more than a decade, I traveled to four or five cities throughout the United States to teach each week. I loved the teaching but loathed the grueling travel and logistics. It was an exhausting way to learn my craft.

As I look back on my career, I realize my first two years in business were not successful because I spent too much time trying to create innovative products, instead of focusing on the speaking/ training side of my business.

My "thy will be done" prayer that one night helped me hear this chapter's wisdom—*Go where you need to grow.* So I put my product aspirations aside and focused on becoming a better speaker/ trainer/teacher. My experience with the seminar company provided more than 10,000 hours of intense, deliberate practice. I taught all day, read my evaluations at night, tweaked my presentations, and tried to deliver a better learning experience for my audience the next day. Things got better because I went where I needed to grow.

After a decade of contracting with the seminar company and slowly building my own client base, I decided to go it alone. I'm happy to report that the pay was much higher and the travel considerably less.

It's a Long and Winding Road

Have you ever sat in front of the fireplace and begged, "Give me heat, then I'll get the wood to put in?" Of course not. That's crazy. Yet people do it all the time. They long for the pot of gold at the end of the rainbow without traveling the long road to find the gold. We need to gather the wood first, then we can sit by the fire.

Next time you're not sure what's next for you, consider praying "thy will be done." If your surrender is sincere, you will hear the whispers of your soul telling you where to go to grow.

CHAPTER 18

It Is in the Receiving That Meaning Is Made

Kevin said he had seen drug deals go down in front of his family's south-central Los Angeles apartment. It was also common to hear gunshots in the neighborhood. Gang wars were everywhere.

"Why do gangs fight each other so much, Kevin?" I asked.

"It's usually about territory or respect" was his matter-of-fact reply.

"How so?"

"Well, if one gang thinks that their territory or a member of their gang has been disrespected, they retaliate."

"Do you see how crazy that is?"

Kevin wrinkled his brow, "Not really."

R.E.S.P.E.C.T.

Kevin had attended a presentation I delivered to inner-city youth a long time ago. I don't remember much about him, but I do recall the nature of our conversation.

"Kevin, you're telling me that if gang member George gets dissed by rival gang member Rick, George will retaliate against Rick, right?" Kevin nodded. "So really, George is letting someone he doesn't like (Rick) control his (George's) behavior. It's like saying, *I don't like you, but I'm going to let you control what I do.* That's crazy! Why should

George care what Rick says or does? Why doesn't he say, *Screw that guy? I'm not going to let him influence me.*"

If a Tree Falls in the Woods...

This story brings to mind the age-old philosophical question, "If a tree falls in the woods and nobody hears it, does it make a noise?" I think the answer is NO, because noise is made when the sound-wave strikes our eardrums. What one hears is between the ears of the beholder. It is in the receiving that meaning is made. *That's the immaculate reception!*

> « *Lightning makes no sound*
> *until it strikes.* »
>
> MARTIN LUTHER KING

I saw Kevin one more time, a year after our first conversation. Again he came up to me after my presentation.

"Hi Dave. I just want to thank you for the conversation we had about choice and free will last year. About six months ago, one of my friends was shot. I didn't know who did it, but I was so angry I wanted to do something about it. But that's when I realized I would be letting someone I didn't know control my actions. It was hard, but I chose to let it go. My friend has recovered and I'm thankful I made the right decision...thanks to you." We shook hands and he walked away.

I never saw Kevin again. But if I did, I'd thank him for allow-ing me to help one inner-city teenager access his free will. He had learned that it is in the receiving that meaning is made. Instead of playing the blame game, he chose to ask one question: What mean-ing do I choose to give this?

> « *No one can make you feel inferior without your consent.* »
>
> ELEANOR ROOSEVELT

You've read all about freedom and choice in earlier chapters. Yet, I share Kevin's story because I believe we all need to be immunized from a rapidly spreading virus called victim mentality. Victim mentality infects us when we think others, often those we may not respect, can wound us with their words. Please understand that I don't condone morons who rant and rave, spitting vile tirades. I also know that it's important to work through the emotional impact of traumatic events, even calling in mental health professionals when needed. After working through it, we still must move ahead and not become stuck in a victim mentality. I believe the wisdom in Kevin's story can help us do so. His story is not about what others say or do, it's about how we choose to think about what they say or do.

We can be free from victim mentality if we understand this: **What others say doesn't bother us; our thoughts about what they say bother us.** If we don't want to be hurt by their words, we can choose to...

1. Seek first to understand.

2. Love our neighbor.

3. Forgive them, for they know not what they do.

4. Forget about them, for they're not worth our time.

5. Proclaim, *I choose to use my free will to hear their free speech.*

6. Recall that sticks and stones may break my bones, but words shall never hurt me.

To think and speak freely is the essence of democracy. So, let others say what they will. If they try to hurt you with their words, inoculate yourself by thinking of one or more of these six wise statements.

CHAPTER 19

A Setback Is Feedback Waiting for Meaning

I needed to complete a three-month internship to satisfy the requirements for graduate school. I chose to go to the University of California–San Diego and work with world-renowned scientist Vic Froelicher, MD, and his team. About six weeks after I started my internship, Dr. Froelicher's research director, Doug, summoned me to his office and bluntly stated, "Dave, we are thinking of firing you."

My shocked brain froze. "What? Why?"

Doug explained, "You don't seem to be getting along with the rest of the team. Figure it out, or we're going to kick you out."

As I shuffled out of his office, my first thought was…OK, I can't print my first thought. My second thought was, *How bad must I be? I'm working for free!*

I can laugh now, but at the time, being rejected by my peers was devastating. How could someone who always had good relationships with everyone, voted Mister Personality in high school, be so unpopular? I didn't understand. I cried myself to sleep that night.

The *Why* Behind the *What*

After a few days of pouting, I mustered the nerve to ask one of the friendlier researchers, Ed, what I was doing wrong. He pointed out the difference in communication styles between the East and West coasts. Ed said I needed to dial back my Connecticut bluntness and embrace a more laid-back California style. He suggested that I listen more, talk less, and ask more questions.

As discussed earlier, the *why* behind the *what* is often unknown. We don't always know why sh*t happens. It's also wise to recall that although setbacks are a given, how we handle them is a choice. Free will empowers us to think of our setbacks as feedback. And the dictionary defines feedback as information returned to the source. Thus, by definition, feedback is neutral. It is just information waiting for us to give it meaning.

It would have been easy for me to blame others for judging me when Ed gave me his feedback. But I didn't. Instead of pointing fingers, I looked in the mirror. I made meaning out of my setback by accepting their feedback. I realized I needed to adapt. *If I wanted to be liked by them, I needed to be more like them.*

The Stories We Tell

What stories do you tell when you face daily difficulties or major setbacks? When you're late for a Zoom call, do you tell a story about your crazy schedule? If you didn't get that promotion, do you point fingers at your boss?

Things got better at UCSD because I chose to see my setback as feedback waiting for meaning. With Ed's help, I started telling myself a story about the East Coast guy in a West Coast world who needed to adapt his communication skills. I was not fired from my internship at UCSD. In fact, at the end of my three months, Dr. Froelicher hired me. A year later, Doug left, and I was promoted to research coordinator. I spent five wonderful years working with

Dr. Froelicher and his terrific team, many of whom are still friends, four decades later.

My circumstances improved because Ed helped me change my story from being a victim (i.e., WOE is me) to learning from setbacks. (i.e., WOW, it's up to me). What's your story?

CHAPTER 20

The Future Always Begins Today

Glory Days

A talented guitarist and his band played the clubs on the Hollywood strip during the 1980s. Musicians told me this guy should have made it to the top of the charts, but too many drugs and too little practice doomed his career. The last time I saw him, he was in poor physical, financial, and emotional health. He spent our entire lunchtime reliving his "glory days" on Sunset Boulevard. His yesterday consumed the day.

Whenever we overfocus on the past, we miss the present. And isn't the present what life is? The *past* was. The *future* isn't. Our *now* is. That's why the gift of life *is* the present.

Think about an incident that happened to you. It doesn't matter when it happened or what it was; I just want you to think about some event or experience for a minute. Come on, this is an interactive book. I'll wait until you come up with something to ponder. Now, think about it for one full minute. Create the vivid sights, sounds, and feelings you had at that time. Please do this for one full minute.

> « *It's okay to look at the past,*
> *just don't stare.* »

BENJAMIN DOVER

Now, what did you miss as you thought about the past? Of course, you missed what was happening in the present while you contemplated something from your past. When we spend time in the past, we miss the present. Not that it's always bad to go back in time. We can't learn from the past unless we think about it at times. And reminiscing is fine, as long as the past doesn't hold us back.

Let It Go...

When you feel your past is weighing you down today, try this little exercise:

- Imagine there is a raging river in front of you. Create the vivid pictures, sounds, smells of this river rushing right before you.

- Take your baggage (attachments, burdens, disempowering stories) and release it to the river rapids with love. Watch, hear, and feel the river sweep your baggage away. Take a deep breath as you bid your burden goodbye and say, *I release, and I let go.* If your luggage is too heavy, ask someone to help you. (If your baggage is overwhelming, seek a mental health professional.)

- Write on a Post-it note or a three-by-five card: *Yesterday ended at midnight.*

Several years ago, a grandmother told me that she adapted this technique by imagining that she was on a cruise ship, throwing her unwanted baggage (including her husband :-) overboard.

Use this visualization exercise to help you detach from your past difficulties, painful memories, or challenging events. It has worked for me on more than one occasion, but not always the first time. I have needed to be patient with myself and the process. So, repeat this exercise as often as you feel the need to.

We can all learn from the past, but we shouldn't live there like my old guitarist friend does. The future only begins today if we don't let the past steal our present.

CHAPTER 21

People Don't Care How Much You Know Until They Know How Much You Care... About What They Care About

Sara was an executive who marched briskly down the main corridor at 9:05 a.m. One of Sara's direct reports, Sam, could barely keep up with her as he explained his concerns about a project that was in trouble. Sara listened and glanced at her cell phone a few times while acknowledging Sam's concerns. When they reached the conference room, Sara gave Sam a quick recommendation, agreed to follow-up with him, and then ducked into the meeting room five minutes late. Sam shuffled down the hallway, shoulders slumped, and wondered, *What just happened?*

The High Price of Not Paying Attention

During their brief corridor conversation, Sam later told me that he felt that Sara didn't seem to care enough about what was important to him to give him her full attention. Sara didn't realize that her poor listening skills would come back to haunt her in the form of employee disengagement and lost productivity.

You see, Sara was trying to multitask as she and Sam rushed down the hallway. I say she was trying to multitask because neuroscientists have shown that our brains don't really multitask; they merely sequence rapidly. As hard as we try and as much as it seems we can, our brains have a tough time focusing on two things at once. When we try, our IQ drops significantly. That's why multitasking is not a wise way to work.

You can prove this to yourself by conducting a quick thought experiment. Pretend you're driving down a lonely street, listening to a podcast, the news, or whatever your listening pleasure is. Suddenly, a car pulls out in front of you. You slam on the brakes and shout, *"What the F*&^*%R&$&*!!!"* as you stop just in time to avoid an accident. After the other car disappears around the corner, your heart rate slows down, you breathe a sigh of relief, and decide to go back to driving and listening to your program. What are your first thoughts? *What did I miss? Where was I?*

My Rolling University

I have listened to thousands of hours of audio programs in my car, especially when I worked as a salesperson and drove about 700 miles per week. To make use of all that drive time, I turned my car into a rolling university. I listened to so many educational programs that our learning manager gave me permission to order any audio programs I wanted. If I liked it, he bought it. Listening while driving was not difficult for me when the traffic was flowing. I think I may have been able to multitask a bit because driving demanded little focus. (I used to fold laundry on the weekends as I talked to Mom too.) But as soon as driving conditions changed (traffic jam, wet roads, an accident), my brain tuned out the learning and focused only on the driving. I had to constantly revisit what was said on the audio program because road conditions "demanded" my brain's complete attention.

Say It Again, Sam

What happens in cars occurs in organizations all the time. Consider Sara and her direct report Sam as they marched down the corridor side-by-side. Sara was checking her cell phone and thinking about her upcoming meeting while trying to listen to Sam's concerns. Her inefficient corridor conversation created the need for a subsequent "clarification." Sara has yet to learn that giving partial attention costs more than paying full attention.

Great communicators care about what others care about by listening 100%, not 80% or 50%. Consider giving others your full attention because…*they don't care how much you know until they know how much you care…**about what THEY care about.** (The first part, "People don't care how much you know until they know how much you care," is credited to former US president Teddy Roosevelt. The second part, "about what THEY care about," is my contribution.)

No one demonstrated this wisdom as well as Fred Rogers. If you want to see how to connect with others by *caring about what they care about,* watch *Mister Rogers' Neighborhood* (his TV shows) or the movie, *A Beautiful Day in the Neighborhood.* Mister Rogers showed he cared by taking four super-simple steps. Our caring will shine through too if we:

1. Place our attention on our intention before our communication.
2. Make eye content, not mere eye contact.
3. Don't say, "I understand." It doesn't make others feel understood.
4. Do say, "What I hear you saying is....Do I have that right?"

Sara might not have had to talk with Sam again if she had taken these wise steps. I encourage you to adapt them to grow your communication skills.

CHAPTER 22

Do Not Confuse Broadcasting for Communication

Near the end of an executive team meeting, the senior vice president of operations, Michelle, reviewed a lengthy list of actions her team would communicate as they rolled out the new business software. She concluded her remarks by emphasizing, "If it's worth communicating, it's worth overcommunicating." Her colleagues nodded approvingly as they all filed out of the conference room.

When we were alone, she turned to me wearing a proud smile, "What do you think of our communication plan, Dave?"

I replied softly, "I think you're confusing broadcasting for communicating."

"What?" Michelle snapped back.

Communication Breakdown

I explained that if she wanted employee buy-in to her new business software, she needed to recognize that broadcasting is about sending information, while communicating is about sending *and* *receiving* information. Broadcasting is *transmitting*. Communicating is *exchanging*. If she was interested in how her messages were received or acted on, she needed to communicate more and broadcast less.

« Information is not transformation. »

As the only member of our neighborhood association board of directors who has taught goal setting, I recently spent several minutes explaining why we needed to be more focused on strategic goals. My fellow board members seemed to agree, but they didn't seem fully engaged. There was minimal discussion and no commitment to a specific date for a follow-up goal-setting session. I now realize I lectured too much and facilitated too little. I broadcasted when I should have communicated. When do you do that?

Ready, Fire, Aim?

Speaking of goals, we tend to broadcast when we should communicate if we don't define our goal before sending a message. We forget that simple sage advice: *It's easier to hit a target when we have one!* The command is NOT *ready, fire, aim;* it is *ready, aim, fire!* To be ready is to have a goal in mind. To aim is to have that goal in sight. To fire is to shoot at the target. When we fire before we aim, we usually end up shooting ourselves in the foot. That's what I did at our board meeting.

The time to broadcast is when our aim is to "get the word out" (by text, e-mail, podcast, memo, a speech). It's best to communicate when we want to learn how our message is received (using interviews, surveys, focus groups, open-door policies, suggestion boxes). Many times, it's appropriate to do both.

Michelle was smart but unwise. She didn't add communicating

to her leadership toolkit. She just kept on broadcasting. Her major initiative limped along, over budget and behind schedule. Her frontline employees told me that they felt they had no voice in what she was doing, and that this new business software was shoved down their throats. Perhaps if Michelle communicated more and broadcast less, she would not have been fired.

We all send messages throughout our day. It's wise not to confuse broadcasting for communicating when we send them.

CHAPTER 23

A Journey Begins on Common Ground

« *Friends, Romans, countrymen,*
lend me your ears;
I come to bury Caesar,
not to praise him.... »

MARC ANTONY

As the drama unfolds in Shakespeare's *Julius Caesar,* Brutus gives Marc Antony permission to speak at Caesar's funeral IF Antony doesn't blame Brutus for Caesar's death. Antony, Caesar's friend, begins by playing to the crowd's dislike of Caesar's recent actions ("I come to bury Caesar, not to praise him") and approval of Brutus's reasons for killing Caesar. But as the speech unfolds, Antony slowly turns the crowd's attention to Caesar's good qualities ("When that the poor have cried, Caesar hath wept"). By the end of the speech, Antony has painted such a positive picture of Caesar that the crowd became infuriated that Brutus murdered him.

Antony understood that if he wanted others to be on his side, he needed to go to them first. Ron Arden, a presentation coach, once put it this way: *"There are ten laws of great presenting; know thy audience are the first seven."* To know your audience allows you to show your audience you empathize with them. You're on their side and share common ground. When you are with them, you have earned the right to take them on a journey with you. This is the magic of Marc Antony's effective soliloquy.

How Do You Spell Relief?

I recently listened to a politician begin her speech by lamenting what a mess things are in the United States. Like Marc Antony, she showed her audience that she understood their pain: the failing factories, lost jobs, unfair competition....She connected with them by going to them. She then went on to explain how she was the aspirin for their pain. *Vote for me, and I'll set you free.* I didn't fully agree with what she said but applauded *how* well she said it. She knew that *a journey begins on common ground.*

Even though you may not give many speeches, consider how to apply these words of wisdom to your daily interactions—your conversations, meetings, reports, e-mails, texts, social media posts. Do you listen to reply or to understand? Do you get carried away with what you want to say? Do you try to get a feel for the lay of *their* land?

If you want others to buy into your ideas, goals, or plans, go to them like Marc Antony and the politician did. Show others that you know where they're coming from. Here's how you might want to test-drive this idea: Before your next interaction with a friend, team member, boss, or spouse, answer this one question: *How will I show them that I'm with them from the very start?* Select one of your answers to start your conversation. I think you'll find your interaction goes well because you began the journey on common ground.

CHAPTER 24

Increasing Engagement Increases Commitment

The Case of the Reluctant Participant

Pat sat in the back row, her arms folded across her chest, with a scowl on her brow. I thought, *She's not buying what I'm teaching. But why? What's her problem?*

It was the beginning of a two-day leadership workshop, and I was presenting a summary of my participant survey results to the class. My opening PowerPoint slide described the problems they had told me they were experiencing when I conducted one-on-one interviews. I explained that our two days together would address the very issues they had shared with me.

Of the fifteen participants, only scowling Pat, who sat in that back, seemed disengaged. As I was about to move on to the next slide, Pat raised her hand and exclaimed, "You didn't interview me. So I'm having a hard time agreeing with your summary of our challenges."

Pat had been hired two weeks before this workshop. Her department manager told me that Pat didn't have a grasp of the issues on this team. She suggested that I not interview Pat. So, I didn't. Big mistake. In retrospect, I should have interviewed her the same as I did everyone else. It would have been easy to analyze the data knowing Pat was a recent hire. So, what would you do if you were me? Here's how I responded to her outburst.

"Pat, thanks so much for sharing your concern. I messed up and apologize. I should have interviewed you. I made a mistake and I'm sorry. As you look at this list of issues on the screen, are there any you want to discuss? Or do you want to add to this list?"

She answered no, acknowledged that my summary was an accurate description of their issues, and agreed to move on with the workshop. Next time you want to boost buy-in to your presentation, project, or plan, apply the wisdom of the sage who says you should engage.

The Illusion of Inclusion

A few years ago, I was preparing for another presentation by interviewing several senior officers of a large association. I discovered that any member of their association could join any of their two dozen subcommittees. One senior officer even bragged that their inclusion policy created many subcommittees with more than fifty members. When I interviewed the rank-and-file members, I asked them if they felt included in the subcommittees. They responded, Yes! But when I asked them if they felt engaged in the subcommittees' work, they said, No!

I informed the association president, Cliff, that many of the members on these committees had told me that they were frustrated by their limited opportunities to contribute. One member summed it up well: "Inclusion means I'm on the bus, but just along for the ride. Engagement means I have a say about where our bus is going and how we get there." Ironically, this association's emphasis on inclusion limited its members' engagement.

I advised Cliff to conduct an experiment by creating a few sub-committees with only a dozen or so members. These smaller sub-committees could then be asked to develop their own process of reaching out to ask for members' opinions (e.g., through voting, surveys, phone interviews, Zoom meetings, anonymous suggestions). The idea was to help them experience the benefits of engaging members, not merely including them. Last I heard, Cliff had not tried this small experiment. He still suffered from the illusion of inclusion.

The Wisdom in This Lesson

Al, a wise senior vice president of a global construction firm, told me during a recent coaching session that he was upset that his boss, the firm's president, had announced a new human resources policy without any input from Al or his colleagues. Although Al could not undo what the boss did, I asked if his boss's dumpster fire might bring any wisdom to light.

Al correctly pointed out that the incident reminded him that *increasing engagement increases commitment.* When I asked him why this was true, he pointed out that when people are engaged, they usually see how and why certain decisions are made. Understanding the process increases their commitment. Bingo!

« *If they don't believe in the process, they won't believe in the outcome of the process.* »

Next time you want others to commit to your goals, engage them, don't just include them. As you do, let them see your decision-making process. How surprised will you be when you see their strong commitment to your goals?

CHAPTER 25

Treating Everyone the Same Is Not Fair

He stood behind me, grabbed my underwear, and yanked up. I howled like a wounded wolf. My mischievous brother had just given me a wedgie in the middle of our elementary school Christmas concert rehearsal.

"You Jensen boys," barked Ms. D, our elementary school music teacher. "Get out and don't come back!"

Brother Bob laughed all the way home from school. He couldn't care less about singing in the chorus. I cried because I couldn't care more.

I lumbered down the stairs when I got home, knowing I'd find Mom in the basement folding laundry. Startled by my tear-stained cheeks, she asked, "What's the matter, honey?"

I poured my ten-year-old broken heart out. "Ms. D. kicked us both out because Bobby gave me a wedgie during chorus practice."

The Day My Music Died

"Well, if you want to sing, you march back to see Ms. D. tomorrow and apologize for disturbing the rehearsal. Tell her that your brother will not come back, but that you would love a second chance. Ms. D. will let you back into the chorus."

The next day, I shuffled into the music room, head down, my tail between my legs. "Ms. D," I stammered, "I'm sorry I screamed yesterday when my brother gave me a wedgie. He's not coming back, but can I *please* come back and sing again?"

"No! Get out and stay out!," was her shocking command.

That's the day my music died. More accurately, it went dormant in me for fifty years.

If you polled all four of my siblings, they would all tell you Ms. D. was either Cinderella's evil stepmother or the Wicked Witch of the West. Even my angelic sister thought Ms. D was the devil.

Did you ever have a lousy teacher? Think about them for a second. What did they do or not do that made them awful? Reflect on the qualities that made them so bad.

Now, contrast your lousy teacher with one that you loved. I had many great teachers throughout my education. Some of them (Ms. Cole, Ms. O'Brian, and Mr. Smith) even inspired me to attain my teaching degree. (My undergraduate degree is in education.) What about you? I bet you have had great teachers too. Think about one of the best teachers you had. What skills or behaviors did they show that made them so good in the classroom?

I Don't Intend to Offend

As you contrast your terrible teacher with your great one, *do you think it's fair to compensate them equally?* Please understand that I am not against unions. I am for fairness. Treating all teachers the same makes as much sense to me as paying everyone in each profession (e.g., athletes, musicians, lawyers, physicians, salespeople) the same, regardless of the quality of their work. Isn't that crazy? Shouldn't equal pay be compensation for equal work?

« Mediocrity does not deserve
an equal voice with high quality. »

Fifty years ago, I let one lousy teacher silence my song. Kicking both my brother and me out (treating us both the same) wasn't fair. Bobby should have been kicked out and I should have been given a second chance. To my knowledge, Ms. D was never held accountable for her soul-crushing impact on children. The teaching profession treated her and other poor teachers the same way it treated the many outstanding teachers.

Why not celebrate equity, not conformity, by brainstorming answers to this question: *How will I treat others fairly today?*

PS: My wife surprised me on my sixtieth birthday with the gift of singing lessons.

CHAPTER 26

Leaders Unleash the Energy of Others Toward Worthy Goals

My Dinner With Andy

Andy didn't know that his colleagues were so frustrated with him that they had asked me to invite him to dinner. They wanted me to convince Andy to accept my coaching. As dinner salads were served, I asked Andy to describe his first few months as a newly elected city council member. At once, he started complaining about his fellow council members and how their priorities were not aligned with his.

When he finished his woe-is-me rant, I asked, "Andy, do you need the support of your colleagues to deliver on the promises you made to your voters?"

"Yes, I guess that's true," he sighed.

"Look, Andy, I have coached most of your colleagues and the mayor. I have good relationships with them. I understand their priorities and their diverse leadership styles. Knowing where they are coming from can help you get where you want to go. The mayor has already approved a coaching agreement. Let me help you serve your constituents. What do you say?"

Andy shrugged his shoulders and muttered he would think about it. We went on to discuss several political and leadership issues that evening. As we were about to leave, he asked this wise question: "We've talked a lot about leadership, Dave, but I'm a politician. Isn't there a difference?"

"That's a good question, Andy. I think most politicians want to keep their jobs, just like the rest of us. That's why their primary goal is usually to *get reelected*. Based on my research and experience, a leader's top priority should be to unleash the energy of others toward worthy goals. If you and I work together, I think I can help you be both by becoming a better political leader."

My dinner with Andy did not result in a coaching agreement. It's too bad and a bit sad because I think had we worked together, it would have resulted in a win for him, other council members, the mayor, the citizens, and me. Imagine that, a win-win-win-win-win!

Leading Some of the People

You might think that you are not a leader. Maybe not. But don't you influence people, at least to some extent, at home or work? If you affect some of the people some of the time, you are a leader. That's because leadership:

- Is not a title, position, or place on the organization chart
- Is not about the number of direct reports
- Is about motivating others
- Is about communicating credible goals

There is wisdom in thinking about leadership this way because, although you may not have a traditional leadership role, you do influence colleagues, friends, and family. Consider what others see when you're in meetings, conversing with loved ones, or engaged in a hobby. What they see is how you lead.

You can increase your wisdom as you lead at work and home by answering this question throughout your day: *How can I unleash the energy of others toward worthy goals right now?* You might find it helpful to write that question on a three-by-five card or a Post-it note in the morning. Put it in your pocket and answer it whenever you touch the card during the day. Or add a note in your smartphone.

I wish I had worked with Andy and helped him grow his political leadership skills. He would have learned that *the management of tension is the essence of growth,* which just happens to be the focus of the next chapter.

CHAPTER 27

Managing Tension Is the Essence of Growth

If you saw me three minutes after my very first sales call, you would have seen me walking on a cloud with a straight back, head held high, and a proud smile on my face. I was delighted that I just had the opportunity to share my medical and computer knowledge with the prospective customer. We even discussed some of my published research articles, which he had read. *Wow! What a great first sales call.* I was grinning to myself as I crossed the hospital parking lot to my car.

Take a Deep Breath

Before getting into my car, you would have also seen me thank my colleague Joe for joining me on my virgin sales call. Joe was a top salesperson and a friend. When I asked for his feedback about the call, you would have heard this: "Dave, on your next call, make sure the customer can actually see you **take a breath!** You were a machine-gun blabbermouth during this call. The customer couldn't talk much because you wouldn't stop talking. You need to learn that telling is not selling."

Joe's rebuke took the wind out of my *sale.* I was hurt, but I knew he was right. (If it wasn't true, it wouldn't hurt.) My first sales call was a disaster because I couldn't manage the tension between the past and the present. I enjoyed the previous five years of conducting medical research at UCSD Medical Center. When I felt nervous during this sales call, I defaulted to my comfort zone, which was talking about my medical research instead of discussing the customer's needs. Holding onto yesterday was keeping me from serving clients today.

How about you? When do you cling to the security of the past to avoid the anxiety of growth? Does holding on ever hold you back?

The Paradox of Growth

Transitioning from academia to sales was hard for me. After my fateful first sales call, I chose to go on a learning binge. I attended several sales courses. I listened to thousands of audio programs on sales, success, and achievement as I drove from hospital to hospital. I also found it enormously helpful to go on hundreds of sales calls with my colleagues.

It took time to digest all that new information. Like a toddler learning to walk, I kept looking back as I stumbled forward. I have since learned that I was experiencing what's called *the paradox of growth*. As mentioned previously, a paradox is when we have two goals pulling us in opposite directions at the same time. We mismanage the paradox of growth when we cling to the old while rejecting the new.

One of the audio programs, I don't recall which one, stressed the importance of creating a development plan to achieve business goals. So I took that advice and discovered I could manage the tension between the old and new by creating a step-by-step sales plan. Instead of "out with the old and in with the new," I chose to manage the tension between these two. The plan was a blueprint that showed me how to use my UCSD research (the old) and ask great sales questions (the new). My plan provided the stability I needed to manage the change I wanted. Managing this paradox of growth was instrumental in my becoming a top salesperson. It can help you achieve your goals too…just like it did for George Washington.

By George, He's Got It

During the American Revolution, the British army marched in line and in open fields, waiting for orders to fire. George Washington's army scampered among bushes and hid behind trees, firing at will. The British generals did not adapt to Washington's wise ways. They didn't manage the tension of growth. The British clung to their OLD way of fighting (stability) and rejected the NEW (change). Generals who embrace the stability of yesterday but dismiss the reality of today will always be fighting the last war.

Hold On…Loosely!

Managing the tension of growth can help individuals, organizations, and nations. During tumultuous times of change, people often cling to the stability of the past, much like I did during my early sales calls. The paradox of growth teaches us that if we want people to embrace change, we need to give them stability. Stability comes in many shapes and sizes, such as developing detailed plans, communicating a clear vision, living the values we say we believe, creating a sense of urgency for change, engaging key stakeholders early in the change process, and discussing what's not changing.

« God, grant me the serenity
to accept the things I cannot change;
courage to change the things I can;
and wisdom to know the difference. »

SERENITY PRAYER

Next time you or those you care about feel overwhelmed by change, instead of clinging to the past, brainstorm answers to this paradox: *What will give me the stability I need to embrace this change?*

CHAPTER 28

Agility Is the Ability to Respond Flexibly in a Changing Environment

Don't Shoot Jensen

"Don't shoot! Don't shoot!" That's what I shouted at my teammates as I dribbled the basketball and watched the game clock count down from ten, nine, eight seconds. If I dribbled the ball for the next eight seconds, our team would win the championship by one point. With seven seconds left, an opposing player, Bob, lunged to foul me intentionally to stop the clock. I shot the ball, knowing if Bob fouled me while I was shooting, I would get two free-throws. But Bob didn't foul me, and I missed the shot. To make matters worse, Bob grabbed the rebound, dribbled the length of the court, and scored the winning basket. I lost the championship game and earned the nickname "Don't Shoot Jensen."

One of the reasons I lost that game five decades ago was that I failed to demonstrate agility—*the ability to respond flexibly in a changing environment.* Instead of dribbling the ball myself, which was not my strength, I should have been flexible enough to pass the ball to our point guard Chuck. He was the player who could and should have dribbled the final ten seconds of the game for our team.

How agile are you? Do you ever get stuck in the same pattern, unable or unwilling to adjust course, especially when stressed? What's the cost of your rigidity?

Wisdom teaches us that the most successful people and organizations strive to be more agile. If you want to improve your ability to respond flexibly, answer these five questions as you embark on any journey:

1. Where do I need to be more agile?

2. Why is this important?

3. What are the steps needed to get from here to there?

4. How will I applaud progress?

5. Who can help?

After losing that championship game my junior year in high school, I increased my agility by practicing a lot during the off-season (and addressing the five questions, at least subconsciously). And yes, we won the championship the next year. Yahoo! But that hasn't stopped my friends from occasionally calling me Don't Shoot Jensen. :)

CHAPTER 29

Contrast Is How We See

It's a sunny day here in LA and the stars are shining. No, not the Hollywood movie stars. I'm talking about the stars in space. Of course, we can't see them during the day. Stars are seen at night because contrast is how we see.

Contrast is also how organizations sell products, services, and ideas. Consider how television commercials often begin by highlighting a problem, such as stains on our clothes, a disaster striking our home, or the pains of a medical condition. Commercials start this way because advertisers know that pain seizes the brain's attention. Next, they show us how their product relieves our discomfort. Images of clean clothes, satisfied and well-insured homeowners, or pain-free living flash before us. Advertisers use the gap between our present pain (current state) and the pain relief (desired state) to motivate us to buy. Contrast fuels the fire of desire.

Politicians have also mastered the power of contrast. Next time you listen to a politician's speech, notice how they first lament how dreadful things are. They sing the song of *woe is we*, wailing on and on about victims, suffering, and misery. After which, they focus our attention on their prescription for our pain.

The Error of Their Ways

The principle of contrast is neither good nor bad. How we use it makes it so. I use contrast to help potential clients see the merits of hiring me. During the first stage of my consulting process, I ask questions that will help me understand where clients are hurting. For example, a few months ago, I interviewed several leaders and discovered that the organization seldom provided quality feedback to its employees. So, I asked these leaders questions about their cumbersome performance reviews, high employee turnover, and low employee engagement. I wanted to know if their failure to follow feedback best practices had any negative consequences. If the answers were no, they didn't need me. But their responses were yes. I then asked questions to understand what it might look like if we addressed their issues together.

My questions served as a magnifying glass, first focusing the leaders on the pain of their poor practices and then on the benefits of alleviating that pain with my prescription. Only when they felt this contrast were they motivated to hire me. Contrast helped them see! It can do the same for you.

*« People are motivated
for their reasons, not yours. »*

Next time you want others to buy into what your advocating (products, services, plans, ideas, values), apply the wisdom of contrast by taking these four steps:

1. Learn about their current circumstances.

2. Ask about their concerns.

3. Explore the pain they might experience if their concerns are not addressed.

4. Invite them to tell you how they will feel if they followed your recommendation.

The Superpower of Persuasion

The wisdom of contrast helps others feel the pain of distance between where they are (current state) and where they want to be (future state). It is the superpower of persuasion. Use it for good.

« *If unique is what you seek, don't be meek.*
You will find much pleasure in this rule,
but in your boldness, don't be a fool. »

CHAPTER 30

Knowing Where You're Going Doesn't Get You There

Suppose you and a friend are driving along the winding country roads of the White Mountains in New Hampshire. As you journey through quaint New England towns, soaking in nature's fantastic fall foliage, your cell phone loses its signal and your map app dies. You ask your "copilot" to set up the satellite-based GPS so you can find your way to your destination. They respond, "I thought you packed it in your luggage. I don't have it. Sorry."

We seldom get *where* we want to go if we don't know *how* to get there. To journey through unfamiliar terrain trying to reach a destination without a map (or GPS) is like building a house without blueprints—it's a prescription for disaster, well-illustrated in the hilarious movie *The Money Pit*. It took me years to figure out that *knowing where you're going doesn't get you there.*

The Biggest Loser

I've been an avid goal setter for forty years. I have set many goals and am proud to have achieved many, but not all, of them. In fact, when I was an executive at UCLA, I felt like a loser whenever my team and I did not reach our goals. How could a dedicated, goal-oriented person like me miss his targets? I decided to find out.

I began to investigate how the most successful people in a variety of occupations achieved difficult goals. I spent the next ten years poring over thousands of research publications, trying to discern how peak performers in diverse disciplines accomplished their dreams. My first simple, but not simplistic, revelation was this: **High achievers write SMART goals and create detailed plans to reach them.**

Make a New Plan, Man

You might be asking, *What? Goals and plans? That's it?* But wait, there's more....I further discovered that there are three major goal groups:

1. Goal *deniers.* They wander through life, like driftwood on the open sea, not knowing where they're going. They usually end up crashing against rocky shores.

2. Goal *setters.* They write goals but don't always know how to achieve them. When the winds of adversity blow them off course, they have no plan or map to get back on track. When the going gets rough, goal setters get lost.

3. Goal *getters.* They write goals and detailed plans to achieve them. They are the captains of their souls because they know where they are going and how to get there. When the storms hit, goal getters have maps to get back on track.

The importance of creating detailed plans to reach goals was confirmed by the research I conducted with Zig Ziglar (a great motivational speaker) and Ed Locke (the academic father of goal setting).

We discovered that when people set *difficult goals*, writing them down did not predict success. Wait! What? Yes, you read that right! When the going gets tough, knowing where you're going doesn't get you there.

> « *If you fail to plan,*
> *you are planning to fail.* »
>
> BENJAMIN FRANKLIN

Specifically, our research revealed that life satisfaction, income, and overall happiness were higher in only those who *wrote difficult goals AND had plans* to reach them. Because written plans predict success in so many areas of life, I thought it wise to embark on the second part of the journey: discovering the universal elements of great plans.

Over several years, I filled twelve legal notepads summarizing the research on effective plans. The culmination of my long voyage is the Science of Success Equation (see below). It states that **the probability of reaching any SMART goal is equal to the product of commitment times belief times feedback.** If these three keys are not part of the plan, the chances of getting from here to there are slim to none.

The Science of Success Equation

SMART Goals = Commitment × Belief × Feedback

COMMITMENT is the willingness of key stakeholders to overcome the obstacles that impede our progress toward our SMART goals. That's why researchers measure commitment by the actions people take in the face of adversity. In fact, you can gauge anyone's level of commitment by the effort they exert to overcome the obstacles encountered as they strive to reach a difficult goal. Haven't you heard people declare their commitment to a goal, only to see them quit when they hit a bump in the road? High achievers will crawl over broken glass to reach their destination. They don't confuse compliance for commitment.

To strengthen your commitment to any difficult goal, brainstorm answers to this question with key stakeholders: **What are the benefits of achieving this goal?**

> « *If they don't commit, they're going to quit.* »

BELIEF is the second key to an effective plan. The specific belief is called "self-efficacy." It is *an individual's belief in their ability to take the steps necessary to reach their goal.* When I started my business many years ago, I had a written goal and a strong commitment to success. But the sad truth was that I often heard a little voice in my head reminding me that I had no idea what steps would lead me to success. I felt as if I was racing down a mountain on a stormy night, in the dark, with my headlights off.

My ongoing research on the Success Equation taught me that one of the best ways to boost self-efficacy was to model those who had already achieved what I was striving for. So, I joined three professional associations, hired coaches, researched best practices, and followed those who had traveled the road I was merging onto. It took longer than expected, but eventually, I learned the steps that bolstered my belief that I could achieve my goal.

You can boost your belief in your ability to reach any goal by answering this question: *How will I learn the steps needed to achieve this goal?*

FEEDBACK is the third part of great goal-achieving plans. Without feedback, it's too easy to veer off course. We need to ask for frequent, timely, and accurate feedback to assess if we are on track to our goal.

You can prove this to yourself by thinking of an elite performer in any profession (e.g., athlete, musician, physician, lawyer). Go ahead. Think of one peak-performing professional you admire. Now, how much do you think they practiced on their way from good to great? Answer? A lot! Practice, drills, rehearsals are precursors to proficiency. To become excellent in any profession, science says we need about 10,000 hours of progressive practice. And the essence of progressive practice is corrective feedback.

You can use the power of feedback to keep yourself on track by answering this question: *Where can I get the accurate feedback needed to reach my goal?*

The Best-Laid Plans

In this chapter's opening story I shared the memory of driving through the rolling hills of New England with a destination in mind, but we didn't know how to get there. Whenever you pursue a difficult goal, create a plan to boost commitment, build belief, and use feedback to stay on track.

These lessons will help you graduate from goal setter to *goal getter*. Things will keep getting better because you are growing bigger, as explained in the next chapter.

CHAPTER 31

Don't Tell Me What to Think, Teach Me How to Decide

To be wise is to judge well. And the essence of good judgment is excellent decision-making. We all make decisions, big and small, all day, every day, throughout life (what to eat, which college to attend, where to live, when to speak up at a meeting, who to let our kids play with, and on and on). You're deciding right now: *Should I keep reading these words or not?* Human beings are, in fact, decision-making machines. The problem is we are not particularly good at it. Researchers tell us that only about one-half of our major decisions produce the outcomes we intended. Is it any wonder that only fifty-two of the original Fortune 500 companies listed in 1955 still operate today? Many of those failed companies were filled with good people who fell into decision-making traps. To avoid their fate, we need an effective and efficient process.

« *When good people perform poorly, fix their process.* »

We can avoid many of the decision-making pitfalls if we turn to philosophy. The word "philosophy" means the "love" (*philo* in Greek) of "wisdom" (*sophia*). Specifically, we will access four branches of philosophy to reveal the four fundamental questions of great decision-making.

I. What are the relevant Facts?

Epistemology is the branch of philosophy investigating the study of knowledge—how do we know what we know? The first question to ask when making any decision is, *What are the relevant Facts?* For example, when confronted by poor-performing employees, supervisors should gather all the facts related to their performance before deciding how to deal with the situation.

II. What are the desired Outcomes?

Metaphysics is the branch of philosophy that addresses universal truths, how those truths relate to the big picture, and the long-term consequences. Thus, the second question to ask when making any decision is, *What are the desired Outcomes (in the short and long term)?* Consider an employee who makes a mistake. Do you look at the error in the context of the employee's overall, long-term performance? Do you consider what your ten-minute and ten-month outcomes should be?

III. With whom should I brainstorm Options?

The president of an association, Marlene, was hiring a senior executive. She preferred to offer the position to an internal candidate, Bill. Unfortunately, Bill was weak in a few areas that Marlene thought were important. I advised Marlene to brainstorm with Bill about how he could improve these skills. Marlene did just that and subsequently hired Bill, who is performing well in his new position. We can avoid the "blinded by your vision" trap by answering the third question of decision-making: *With whom should I brainstorm Options?*

IV. What evidence supports the Decision?

Existentialism, the fourth branch of our philosophical tree, informs us that we are free agents responsible for our choices and consequences. When we choose from the range of options identified in the previous step, we must clarify the criteria we used to decide. Are we sharing our opinion, or do we have data, research, or proof that predicts our decision will achieve the desired outcome? Thus, the final decision-making question: *What evidence supports the Decision?*

Is What You Get What You Want?

These four questions frame a decision-making process that will increase the odds that what you get is what you want as you make decisions.

I coached a vice president who once told me how delighted he was with the work his managers now brought to him. They no longer shuffled into his office and dumped their problems on his desk. Instead, they now marched in with options because he had coached them to answer these four questions.

Peter Drucker, the father of management, reminds us that leadership used to be about having the right answers. Now, it's about asking the right questions. I encourage you to ask the four fundamental questions of a great decision-making process:

I. *What are the relevant* **F***acts?*

II. *What are my desired* **O***utcomes?*

III. *With whom should I brainstorm* **O***ptions?*

IV. *What evidence supports the* **D***ecision?*

To be wise is to judge well. And the essence of good judgment is excellent decision-making. How surprised will you be that your wisdom grows because you now have **FOOD** for thought FULL decisions?

CHAPTER 32

Things Get Better as We Grow Bigger

This is your bonus (leap year) chapter. Enjoy!

• • •

I had three brushes with death before I turned twenty-one. These were not the kind of "near-death experiences" where I was on death's door, hooked up to a life-saving medical machine. No, these were frightening incidents that brought me within a whisker of death without causing any physical injuries. I won't burden you with all the details, but ask that you visualize me in these close encounters:

- Clinging to a Wyoming mountain-ledge for dear life.

- Jumping behind a utility pole that shielded me from getting run over by an out-of-control, careening, crashing car.

- Fishtailing and skidding down a steep, icy mountain road in my black 1961 Dodge Seneca (nicknamed "The Batmobile").

> « *Thinking about death*
> *five times a day brings happiness.* »
>
> BHUTANESE PROVERB

Keep Your Eyes on the Road
AND Your Hands on the Wheel

These three dramatic events were traumatic at the time. Yet now I see how they awoke in me the wisdom in Macbeth's soliloquy, "Out, out, brief candle." I was a teenager comprehending what it means to be a candle in the wind. Learning that death is so near, a mere whisper away, has helped me manage one of life's great paradoxes—to be mindful of this moment AND to think long term. Death taught me to manage the tension in this paradox by answering two questions, which usually led to wise decisions:

- *What do I want to say about this when I'm rocking in my retirement chair?*

- *What do I owe my future self, right now?*

Today's immediate demands are shiny objects that often command immediate attention. But pausing to ponder these two questions whenever we face crossroad moments can keep daily urgencies from overwhelming our long-term priorities. The wisdom of *both/ and* thinking can help you be here now *while at the same time* reflecting on your future.

As our adventure together nears completion, it's time to reflect on the three ways I intended this book to boost your wisdom. First, I hope you apply the FOOD decision-making process to improve the quality and consistency of your decisions. Second, you can now use the wisdom of paradoxical thinking to avoid the pull of instant gratification at the expense of long-term satisfaction. Finally, it was my sincere desire that you glean a few coping skills to help you manage the inevitable pains of life.

Using these three approaches to increase your wisdom should also boost your score on the Wisdom Insight Quiz. Let's find out. Once again, please score the following ten statements on a scale of 1 *(strongly disagree)* to 5 *(strongly agree)*. Don't overanalyze or look at your previous score. Answer them honestly and quickly from your gut:

1. I often feel real compassion for everyone.

2. I frequently laugh at my little mistakes and use humor to put others at ease.

9. I enjoy being around others whose views are strongly different from mine.

4. I have a deep desire to understand the truth.

5. I am not easily irritated by people who argue with me.

6. I like to recall my past to provide perspective on my current concerns.

7. I make important decisions after gathering facts and considering diverse opinions.

8. I often wonder about the mysteries of life and what lies beyond death.

9. I easily express my emotions without losing control.

10. I have learned from many painful events in my life.

WISDOM Is *What I Shall Do On M*onday

1. Add up your answers to generate your wisdom score.

2. Plot your score on the Wisdom Insight Continuum below.

3. Once again, select one low-scoring statement you want to improve.

4. Brainstorm answers to this question: How will I boost my score this time around?

5. Integrate your ideas with those you find as you reread this book.

Unwise	Narrow-minded	Open-minded	Mindful	Wise
10	20	30	40	50

I hope you still see a wisdom gap because we never really arrive. The best we can do is keep growing, adapting, and applying lessons learned. Using what we learn, not sitting on a mountaintop, is wisdom's way because **WISDOM** stands for *What I Shall Do On M*onday. I recommend you choose an accountability partner, or a group at work, and report your weekly progress every Monday.

« *Each of us must work for her own improvement, and at the same time share general responsibility for all humanity.* »

MARIE CURIE

On a moonlit night fifty years ago, I leaned against a giant oak tree in our backyard and opened a book of stories to a random page. The moonlight illuminated Solomon's story and his prayer for wisdom. Thus began my quest for wisdom. I don't know if I found it.

You can be the judge. I have stumbled, fallen, and messed up over the years. I still screw things up at times. But I sojourn on knowing it's what we do after the fall that matters most, after all. I don't get stuck in the muck or give up. I know when it's time to climb back in the saddle again and ramble on. Now, you do too.

See you on the mountain....

« You're the potter and the clay
Molding destiny every day.
Wisdom will shape you as you go
If you pursue what's true and you grow. »

Two More Songs
You May Enjoy

Long to Belong

Stagger home, alone in the dark
Hidden tears drown a spark.
First dance started hours ago
All dressed up, too scared to go.
Shuffled in the hall, head hung low.
Heart sinks as the music grows.
Too many backs, cliques, and groups
Can't dance with girls in private troupes.

> *Long to belong.*
> *A lone feelings so strong.*
> *Friends unlike me, something's wrong.*
> *Can't ya tell me what's going on?*
> *How, tell me how, do I belong?*

Outside again, inside I scream.
Another school, cut from the team.
Dying for a safe way home,
Outcasts pray that bullies don't roam.
Cracks in the mirror on the wall

Distort the truth, feeling small.
If I'm different, is that a sin?
I'm reaching out, I need a friend.

> *Long to belong.*
> *A lone feelings so strong.*
> *Friends unlike me, something's wrong.*
> *Can't ya tell me what's going on?*
> *How, tell me how, do I belong?*

My first job changed it all
I said yes when I got the call.
A leader, mentor, then a friend,
Bob taught me to let go of fitting in.
I learned to serve, think more we.
Focused on others, less on me.
My voice grew strong with each new role.
We climbed mountains, reached tough goals

Next time you feel pushed aside,
Take three steps to turn the tide.
First, serve others where they are.
Helping them heals your scars.
Then set goals, reach sky-high.
Each step up builds you inside.
When you're in, ask who's out?
Shadows need your light to shout

> *We all belong.*
> *YOUnique and YOUnited,*
> *Makes us strong,*
> *To be both isn't wrong.*

So join the dance with your song.
The me-we stretch is going on.

Embrace both me and we
Be the I in team, we see
Life's paradox pulls one and all
To dance alone and with the hall.

Fitting In Made Me Small

Long ago do you recall
How you made me feel so small?
You sold me on fitting in
Not to be the me within

With others, I shrank to be
Who you wanted them to see.
I wasn't strong, I went along
To be with you, I bought your con.

> *Fitting in made me small,*
> *Love in chains binds us all*
> *Doubt drove out my security*
> *I fell for your conformity*

Too tame to walk away
So lame I heard you say:
He's a puppy-dog on my leash
I sat, stayed, followed your lead

> *Fitting in made me small,*
> *Love in chains binds us all*
> *Doubt drove out my security*
> *I fell for your conformity*

One spring morn I was reborn
High above the desert floor.
An epiphany dawned in me
Hear within and you may see:

    As beauty grows deep inside
    Deserts bloom far n wide
    Seeds once stirred by high winds
    Blossom now from within

So don't fit in, don't be small,
Love in you blooms for all
To be real is security
You're an oasis born free